100 Keys for Hope

by Vicki Bennett

Level 3
(1600-word)

IBC パブリッシング

はじめに

　ラダーシリーズは、「はしご（ladder）」を使って一歩一歩上を目指すように、学習者の実力に合わせ、無理なくステップアップできるよう開発された英文リーダーのシリーズです。

　リーディング力をつけるためには、繰り返したくさん読むこと、いわゆる「多読」がもっとも効果的な学習法であると言われています。多読では、「1. 速く 2. 訳さず英語のまま 3. なるべく辞書を使わず」に読むことが大切です。スピードを計るなど、速く読むよう心がけましょう（たとえば TOEIC® テストの音声スピードはおよそ 1 分間に 150 語です）。そして 1 語ずつ訳すのではなく、英語を英語のまま理解するくせをつけるようにします。こうして読み続けるうちに語感がついてきて、だんだんと英語が理解できるようになるのです。まずは、ラダーシリーズの中からあなたのレベルに合った本を選び、少しずつ英文に慣れ親しんでください。たくさんの本を手にとるうちに、英文書がすらすら読めるようになってくるはずです。

《本シリーズの特徴》

- 中学校レベルから中級者レベルまで5段階に分かれています。自分に合ったレベルからスタートしてください。
- クラシックから現代文学、ノンフィクション、ビジネスと幅広いジャンルを扱っています。あなたの興味に合わせてタイトルを選べます。
- 巻末のワードリストで、いつでもどこでも単語の意味を確認できます。レベル1、2では、文中の全ての単語が、レベル3以上は中学校レベル外の単語が掲載されています。
- カバーにヘッドホーンマークのついているタイトルは、オーディオ・サポートがあります。ウェブから購入／ダウンロードし、リスニング教材としても併用できます。

《使用語彙について》

レベル1：中学校で学習する単語約1000語

レベル2：レベル1の単語＋使用頻度の高い単語約300語

レベル3：レベル1の単語＋使用頻度の高い単語約600語

レベル4：レベル1の単語＋使用頻度の高い単語約1000語

レベル5：語彙制限なし

Introduction

The world media focuses on planet earth as an unfriendly, unsafe place, and it sometimes looks that way. In spite of this, the human spirit remains strong, kind, generous, and hopeful. Although there are wars, political turmoil, and pandemics at any given time, I feel more hopeful and confident about the human spirit than ever before.

This book has everything about living a hope-filled life. It offers clear choices, ideas, and inspirations for a good life, and helps readers to build hopeful lives with courage and inspiration. Many of the ideas and tools in this book are about dealing with anxiety. I've found that high levels of anxiety can smother hope in a heartbeat.

I have shared what I have learned about handling the ups and downs in life. As an adult, I've struggled with feeling that I am enough. The need for approval has always driven me, often to the high end of anxiety, and, when I was younger, to depression. Like many others, I have had lots of counseling to help find where my anxiety started, and this journey has helped me to live a life of curiosity, love, and passion.

Each chapter is part of a knowledge map, giving direction and guidance to assist you on your journey toward hope. The messages in each chapter are aimed at creating a positive life and share ideas for living well in this crazy world.

You are not alone; each one of us is searching for hope, love, and self-discovery. This book understands the yearning in each of us and shows the way forward. The tools and skills in the pages of this book will lead you to success and hope.

My deepest thanks to all the people who contributed to this book. A special thanks to Mariko Hyland for your perseverance, and professionalism over three decades as my literary agent in Japan. And thanks to Ian Mathieson for editing this book.

Vicki Bennett

———— ✳ ————

About the Author

Vicki is an author, artist, filmmaker, writing coach, and corporate trainer. She has written 35 books and written and co-produced a documentary, *Never Forget Australia*.

Her writing career began with personal development books and has expanded to children's books, young adult, and adult fiction. Books include: *I've Found the Keys Now Where's the Car?*, *Life Smart*, *The Effective Leader*, *Signposts for Life*, *Two Pennies*, *The Little Stowaway*, *Oliver's First Big Spy Adventure*, *The Book of Hope—Antidote to Anxiety*, *The Flying Angel*, and *The Promise*.

Web: www.vickibennett.com.au
Instagram: vickibennettcreativity
Facebook: vickibennettcreativity

CONTENTS

名言の著者

Chapter 1 **Eleanor Roosevelt** エレノア・ルーズベルト (1884-1962) アメリカ第32代大統領フランクリン・ルーズベルトの妻（ファーストレディ）。夫の死後、1946年から1952年までアメリカの国連代表も務めた。

Chapter 2 **Philo of Alexandria** アレクサンドリアのフィロン（生没年不詳） 古代ローマ帝国のアレクサンドリアで活躍したユダヤ人哲学者。ギリシア哲学をユダヤ教思想に初めて適用し、初期キリスト教思想に大きな影響を与えた。

Chapter 3 **Wayne Dyer** ウェイン・ダイアー (1940-2015) アメリカの心理学者・作家。マズローの自己実現をさらに発展させた「個人」の生き方重視の意識革命を提唱し、新個人主義の旗手として知られている。

Chapter 4 **Miguel Ruiz** ミゲル・ルイス(1952-) メキシコの作家。かつてメソアメリカに存在したとされる伝説のトルテカ帝国の精神主義的、新思想的な教えに着目した著述で有名。

Chapter 5 **Ashleigh Brilliant** アシュリー・ブリリアント (1933-) イギリスの作家・漫画家。1975年からアメリカで発表されている、1コマのイラストに1行のユーモアあるコメントを添えた「Pot-Shots」で知られている。

Chapter 6 **Walt Disney** ウォルト・ディズニー (1901-1966) アメリカのアニメーター・実業家。世界的に有名な「ミッキーマウス」をはじめとするキャラクターの生みの親であり、「ディズニーランド」の創立者。

Chapter 1

Make Peace with Anxiety

I gain strength, courage, and confidence by every experience in which I must stop and look fear in the face.

Eleanor Roosevelt,
US First Lady, Humanitarian.

What is hope?

Hope is optimism with action. It is believing that life is beautiful, even though some of the things that happen in life aren't. And that your life will work out. Hope means being mostly positive about the future.

It's being cheerful, kind, and grateful about what you already have—being more optimistic with colleagues at work, and with family and friends in your personal life.

Hope means that you set goals and create action to make those goals come true. Goals such as being more joyful, grateful, or compassionate will help you to become more hopeful. Actions such as helping someone carry their shopping bags, helping a child to learn, or opening a door for someone who has their hands full; all match a hopeful attitude.

Now, more than ever, is the time to become more hopeful.

2.

Bring hope into your life

Whether you think about it or not, hope is a big part of everyone's life. Everyone hopes for something good to happen.

Hope has many shapes—a happy child, an open door, a new book to read, a lost credit card returned to its owner, a new beginning, or a fresh spring day. It is a feeling of trust, of wanting good things to happen in the future, of hoping your life can be better in some way.

Hope reduces stress and improves your quality of life.

To bring hope into your life, first, you need to have an open, calm, and positive outlook on life. Secondly, you need to do good things to bring hope into your life. Be kind to yourself and others, speak well of others, look for the positive things that are happening around you, and build on these.

3.

Be your best self

Would you like to be the best version of yourself?

The version that is kind, hopeful, generous, and grateful? It is easy to look at others and think they are doing better than you. You don't know if they are. Each of us is dealing with challenges, so it is important to do the best you can.

Your thoughts and actions impact your level of hope. Do small things every day to be your best self, and increase your level of self-care by being more optimistic.

Be kind to yourself and others—go out of your way to do something kind for another person. Listen well, and pay attention to what other people say to you without jumping in. Listening well is a great way to become the best you can be.

4.

Think differently

Humans have been trained for thousands of years to think about the negative. This kept us safe in the past when we needed to be aware of danger and threats. We now still focus on what's going wrong, what's missing, and what might go wrong in the future.

Being more grateful for what you have is a way of building more resilience and strength. Noticing the good things in your life, and the source of those good things, creates a high level of gratitude and is linked to life happiness and hope.

When you take the time to shift your attention to what's working in your life, more of your needs can be met. Gratitude tones down the alarm system in your brain; this reduces your feelings of stress, and creates a feeling of well-being.

Gratitude balances out negativity and builds aware-ness of what you want in your life, rather than what you don't want.

5.

Listen carefully

Everyone loves to be listened to.

When you listen carefully, you become much more valuable to others because they like to feel heard. When someone feels heard, they feel more respected and liked.

It is not just listening to another person until you feel you understand them—it is so that they feel well listened to. A feeling of being understood bonds us to that person. When people feel heard and understood, they feel more valued and hopeful about the future.

When you really listen to someone, they are more likely to seek to listen to you, as listening develops deep trust.

6.

Notice anxiety

Pandemics and wars happen all over the world and are on your screens and in newspapers all the time. These events can make you feel anxious and sad about the state of the world.

Anxiety about work, study, family, and money can also wear you down. You cannot control what happens outside of your life, but if you look after yourself by what you think and believe, you can develop resilience.

When you become aware of anxiety, take deep-diaphragm breaths and focus on something that has happened that was great; then breathe into that feeling. Leaning into positive feelings will help the anxiety to let go of you.

You are stronger than you think you are.

7.

Social media

When you are surfing the web, notice if you start to feel envious or jealous of the people you are reading about. Stop, feel that feeling, and take note of where it lands in your body. Honor that feeling; stay in that discomfort without attaching a story about who's better or what's wrong; just breathe into it.

Let's not be frightened by our feelings; dive into them when the balance of what is happening is tipped in some way. Let's meet them with love and kindness.

Then close your eyes to rest into that feeling, and it will eventually let go of you. Resistance to uncomfortable feelings only causes more anxiety.

8.

Resilience

Having resilience is knowing that not only can you survive the painful and hard parts of your life, but your human spirit can rise above problems.

We're built to bounce back from difficult situations. What stops us from bouncing back is believing that we're not resilient. Some of us come from families where we were taught to believe we are weak and fragile and need looking after.

We are not.

Build your resilience every day by doing something difficult by 10 a.m. The gratitude you will feel from doing this will build your resilience. Resilience is like a muscle—the more you do hard things, the stronger it will grow.

9.

Only swans glide

Do you look calm like a swan on the outside, in control and confident but you are paddling like crazy underneath the water because you can't keep up with the pace of life?

Being calm all the time isn't possible or normal.

Allow yourself to feel other emotions, like scared, hurt, lonely, and afraid. It's OK to feel these things; it is part of being a person. Breathe into these feelings, and don't be afraid. You can deal with them if you allow them to be felt. Then when you have relaxed into these feelings, they will leave you.

10.

Meditate

Meditation is a big part of self-care. There are other ways to relax besides reading and social media. Meditation is about taking some time out from actively doing things all the time.

You can meditate and lessen stress by doing the following.

1. Lie down and relax your body.
2. Close your eyes.
3. Let go of any stress.
4. Uncross your arms and legs.
5. Take some deep breaths; hold each breath for a couple of seconds and let it go.
6. Allow your body to relax.
7. Let thoughts flow through you without stopping or thinking about them.
8. Don't attach yourself to any words or stories you have.
9. Let your body feel calm.
10. Enjoy this feeling.
11. Open your eyes and notice how much better you feel.

Try to stay that way for at least five minutes. Do this once every day.

Chapter 2
Kindness

Be kind, for everyone you meet is fighting a great battle.

Philo of Alexandria,
Philosopher.

11.

Remedy for anxiety

Kindness is a strong remedy for anxiety. Small, nice things you do for yourself and others have a positive impact on your mind, body, and spirit, and tone down feelings of anxiety and stress.

Kindness works because it connects you with hope. When you take the time to be kind, you will be in the present moment, which is a place of power. Thinking too much about the past can create sadness, and thinking too much about the future creates anxiety.

A kind word can give a warm feeling to another person. It also makes you feel good about yourself.

12.

A seed of hope

Every time you do something kind for another person, a tiny seed of hope begins to grow and can affect the other person in ways that you may never find out about.

It's usually small kind things that mean the most to others. Try the following:

- Smile more, even to people you don't know.

- Make a cup of tea for someone else.

- Say something nice to another person.

- Open a door for someone, and let them go first.

- Let the person behind you go before you at the supermarket because they have only one item to buy, and you have a full basket.

Simple things are the best things to do.

13.

Look for the good

When we meet people for the first time, we can be very unkind to them. We can think that they are not good enough for us, or nice enough, or we can think negative thoughts about them.

If you are thinking unkind thoughts about others, you are putting yourself above them, making it impossible to feel connected with them. It is being unkind to yourself, as well as to the other person.

Look for the good in others. Notice things that are kind and nice about them—their smile or voice, the way they talk or stand, or the clothes they wear. Notice what is good about them, and you will connect easily with them.

14.

Stop looking for mistakes

It is easy to notice mistakes in other people, but it takes kindness to find the good things others do and let them know about them.

Being kind to others is something you can do on purpose. It asks you to focus on what's going right with others and helps to build on that. When you are kind to others, the goodness in them is revealed, and this helps them to build on their own goodness.

Kindness to others allows other people to be better than they thought they could be, which builds confidence and love between people.

15.

Acts of kindness

Kindness occurs when you think with more compassion about someone else, than you do of yourself.

Look at the relationships you have created with other people in your life. What have you given to others by way of time, energy, and kindness?

You will get back what you give out in life.

Be kind by giving up your seat on a train or bus to someone who needs it more than you. It could be an older person, a pregnant woman, or a person who looks tired.

When you do this, you build kindness for others and within yourself.

16.

Giving and receiving

The circle of kindness is only complete when you give and receive equally; otherwise, it will be unbalanced. Be gracious when you say something nice to another person.

Also, be gracious when something nice is said to you. Don't say, "Oh, it was nothing," when someone says something kind. Say, "Thank you," smile, and take the nice thing they have said into your heart.

Being kind allows you to feel something greater than yourself, to be a bit better than you are. Everyone can do this; you just have to practice saying, "Thank you."

17.

Nurturing self

Everyone says or does the wrong thing many times in their lives.

When you feel the shame of making a mistake, this is when you need to love, support, and care for yourself the most, opening your heart to yourself for who and what you are in that moment.

When someone is being unkind to another person, this comes from being unhappy, sad, or resentful. That person will most likely have a low view of themselves and is speaking to you as they speak to themselves. Being unkind and treating themselves badly, and then doing it to you, is how they make themselves feel safe.

18.

Choose to learn

When someone is unkind to you, this is the time to learn, not the time to be unkind to yourself as well. Don't join in with the other person by speaking badly to yourself.

Notice how you feel when someone is unkind to you. Notice where you feel this in your body. Stop thinking, and feel where it lands in your body. Stay with that feeling in your body.

Learn to love that part of you that is feeling the unkindness, and just relax. This is where you learn to truly love yourself—the good, bad, and the sad.

19.

Be aware

Awareness is the first step in being kind. Notice small things that give you and other people joy, and do them for yourself and others.

Here are some actions to take to nurture a kind heart:

- Be aware of wonder; notice all the beautiful things around you; like the sun shining, and the birds singing.
- Open your heart to receive kindness.
- Open your heart to give kindness to yourself.
- Pick up the rubbish others leave behind, and dispose of it thoughtfully.
- Treat everyone as if they were part of your family.
- Let someone who is in a hurry go before you.
- Help someone do something that is hard for them.
- Take tea or coffee in bed to someone you live with.
- Be kind to someone to whom it is hard to be kind.
- Speak kindly to yourself for a day, and then repeat that for a week.
- Laugh; share your love of life with others.
- Tell your friends you are grateful for them.

Being aware of all the things you can be grateful for is the way you can improve your kindness.

20.

Make the world a better place

To be kind, you don't have to do something big for others. A small kindness can have a large impact.

Your body will feel better by both giving and receiving kindness. When your body feels good, you can make better choices for yourself, and be clearer about your goals and actions for the future. Kindness is the source for you to become a better child, a better mother or father, a better uncle or aunt, a better friend, or a better person.

When you think about others, it breaks the cycle of anxiety and moves you toward gratitude and hope, and for that moment it makes the world a better place.

Chapter 3
Sacred Service

*You cannot always control
what goes on outside, but you can always
control what goes on inside.*

Wayne Dyer,
Author.

21.

Be brave

If you met yourself on the street, would you greet yourself with kindness and understanding? Why is it that you give others what you aren't prepared to give yourself?

It takes more bravery to care for yourself than it does to care for others. The approval you want is an inside job.

It's lonely being unkind to yourself. When you feel lonely is the time for you to be more compassionate to yourself.

It takes courage to care for yourself.

22.

Find compassion

Don't bully yourself, or shame yourself about what's happening in your life. As soon as you feel you are being unkind to yourself, talk to yourself in a compassionate, loving, and caring way so that you can do better next time.

Focus on being kind to yourself before saving the world. If you are on social media all the time and not looking after your own levels of stress and anxiety, you're going to feel hopeless.

Hope is triggered by the strength and dignity you feel inside. If you want to contribute to saving the world, begin with liking yourself.

23.

Present time

When you think too much about a problem, it can turn to worry in a heartbeat. The things you worry about may have happened days ago, but you may be still worrying about them now.

The key is to let go of thoughts about the past and live in present time. Remind yourself of what you are doing now. You may be sitting in a chair, on a train, at work, or at home. Wherever you are right now is important. Try to bring yourself back to what's happening in this moment.

No one can change the past. Forgive yourself for thinking that your past could have worked out any differently. Let go of what you said or did yesterday, and look at where you are, and what you are doing right now.

The great thing about the past is, it's over.

24.

Notice good things

Next time you go for a walk, notice the small things—the leaves on the trees, the birds singing, the rocks on the path, the blue of the sky, the colors of the flowers—anything that brings you back into mindfulness. To notice these things is healing and very healthy for your body.

Remind yourself to do this every time you leave your home. Take a morning or afternoon walk in nature to help draw soft kindness back into your heart.

The more grateful you are about the things around you, the less likely you are to notice what you don't have.

25.

Feel gratitude

When you wake up every day, feel grateful for what you have, rather than worrying about what you don't have. Don't wait for great things to happen before being grateful.

Be thoughtful about how you speak to yourself about yourself. Be aware of negative thinking about the past, or anxiety about the future, as either can be very painful.

Be happy for the smallest things—sunshine, the view outside, a cup of coffee, a smile, your pet, the way your legs move when you get out of bed, and your family and friends. Be thankful for everything.

When you feel gratitude, you cancel out negativity. Focus on what you want in your life, not on what you don't want. Good memories are formed by noticing what's working and what you are grateful for.

26.

Future worry

Being worried about something that may or may not happen in the future creates a lot of anxiety.

Use deep breathing to lessen anxiety. Take a deep breath in for the count of four; then hold it while you count to four; then breathe out to the count of four. Repeat this five times. You will feel less anxious and calmer.

Bring yourself back into the present moment by searching out three things you can see or focus on. Then notice three things you can smell and three things you can touch. Doing this calms the mind and brings your attention into the moment.

27.

Take time to relax

Are you a relaxed person, or are you stressed all the time? Do you rush around trying to please others, and have no time for yourself?

Many people think that going online will relax them. They surf the web without contributing anything, and they can't understand why they feel lonely instead of feeling connected. Web surfing can trigger feelings of jealousy and anxiety.

There are ways to relax other than watching screens. Take time out from screens by doing the following:

- Have a cup of tea.

- Take a walk in the park.

- Rest on your bed.

- Do a puzzle.

- Read a book.

- Take a break from your work and breathe into this moment.

When you take the time to care for yourself, you are showing yourself and others that you are important too.

28.

Action for self-care

Hope is activated optimism with action. That means you need to do things to create this hope. Self-care is a great way to start.

Here are some ideas to keep beside your bed, where you can be reminded of them daily:

- Let go of wanting to be liked by others.

- Give yourself time to do the things that bring you joy.

- Be kind to yourself when you make a mistake.

- Speak kindly to yourself, as if you were your best friend. Use words like: *I'm OK*, or *Everything will work out.*

- Be clear about what you will and won't do.

- Notice any big or small kind things you have already done.

- Laugh more often.

- Share your happiness with your friends and family.

Self-care means doing these small things every day.

Chapter 4

Power Words

Be impeccable with your words.
Don't take anything personally.
Don't make assumptions.
Always do your best.

Miguel Ruiz,
Author.

29.

Self-talk

What you think and talk to yourself about most of the time has great power over your life. Telling yourself stories about the past or the future does not protect you from future failure or make you safe.

It is the everyday conversation with yourself, which becomes your self-talk, that has the most influence over your thinking. You talk to yourself from the first waking moment in the morning until you go to sleep at night.

You can change your thinking by changing how you talk to yourself. Positive self-talk is saying things to yourself like: *I can solve problems*, *I am a kind person*, *I can do hard things*, *My work is worthy*, *I am good to my family*, *I am kind to my friends*, or *I like myself*.

This self-talk supports you to feel more grounded in present time and helps you to be a more compassionate person.

30.

Stay present

Your mind will go to wherever you lead it. Staying in the present keeps you grounded, and that is where your power is.

If you re-live the past as if it were now, it will stay with you. Negative self-talk is blaming yourself for what's happened in the past and doesn't make anything better. Listen to your self-talk and make sure it is mostly kind, caring, and supportive to you.

We think on average 100,000 or more thoughts a day; many of them are repeats of thoughts we had the day before. When we think new thoughts or create new positive messages, we can change the way our brain works.

Commit to talking with yourself as if you were your best friend, a loved child, or a most valued client.

31.

The words you speak

The words you speak have a big impact on your life.

You don't have to be in danger to feel fear. You can reach the same level of fear when safe in your bed, just by worrying about something you have to do the next day or something you didn't do today.

To move away from fear, use powerful phrases like: *I am calm*, *This is easy*, *That was fair*, *I am happy*, *I can heal*, *I am kind*, *I like myself*, *I am brave*, *This is fun*, *I love to hug*, *I agree*, *I am grateful*, and *I have hope for the future*.

These words encourage positive thoughts and positive relationships with all the people in your life.

32.

I am

I am are often words that come before negative self-talk like: *I am hopeless, I am not good enough, I am stupid, I am tired, I am scared,* or *I am a bad person.*

You need to balance these negatives with positive affirmations like: *I am great, I am good enough, I can do this,* or *I am strong enough to try this.* It's the words that come after *I am* that make our lives successful or not.

We constantly talk to ourselves, from the first bright waking hour to that last sleepy minute of every day. We notice every good and bad thing that is going on around us.

It takes courage to look for the good and reflect this in our self-talk.

We need to use words about our future that tell us what we want to feel. These are our magic wand to a positive future.

33.

Body shape

Women and girls who read magazines or look at online photos of the *perfect* body are often unhappy with their own body shape.

If you are unhappy with your natural shape, your self-talk may be like this: *I am fat*, *I am ugly*, or *I'm not good enough*. These words give your mind a picture of what it is you don't want.

Try saying instead: *I am the right weight for me right now*, *I am beautiful inside and out*, or *I am good enough*.

When you use positive self-talk, it stops the shame, blame, and guilt many women feel about their bodies. It makes more sense to use words that reflect what you want, rather than what you don't want.

34.

The power of positive words

When you are getting ready to meet someone for the first time, or when you give a talk to a group of people, imagine the person or people enjoying what you have to say, and liking you and what you have to say.

Use positive words to talk to yourself such as: *I have everything I need to do a good job, I am safe, I can speak well, I can do a great job,* or *I'm doing well.*

Your self-talk reflects what you want to achieve. Speaking like this to yourself means that you will be the best you can be on that day.

35.

You can fix this

Often, when something happens that is difficult, you may want to call someone to tell them your troubles. We often want to share our problems with others. We do this so that someone else may be able to help us or solve our problems for us.

It rarely happens that they can help us.

Sometimes, when you tell another person about your problems, they may tell you that's exactly what happened to them, and turn the conversation into being all about them. That is not at all helpful.

No one else has the information that you have to solve your problem. You are the best person to fix it. You understand how, when, and why it happened.

You hold the key to solving it.

When you have a problem, find a quiet place to sit and ask yourself, "What advice would I give my friend if they were in the same situation?" then wait patiently until you have the answer.

36.

Build your world with your words

Most of the time it is your negative self-talk that gets in the way of doing something exciting.

Listen to your intuition to direct you to do something, or not to do something. Check with this inner voice rather than listening to your negative self-talk.

Positive self-talk about events and people feeds your self-esteem, which feeds your self-confidence and how you view the world. Positive self-talk makes the world a friendly place.

Commit yourself to communicating in a kind, thoughtful way, using positive self-talk. Let your words enrich and reflect your very best self to build the best possible world around you.

Chapter 5

Values-driven Behavior

At any moment,
I could start being a better person — but
which moment should I choose?

Ashleigh Brilliant,
Author.

37.

Clarify your values

If you met someone for the first time and they asked you, "What are your values in life?" what would you answer?

Work out what you value and what is important to you. You use your values in every part of your life — in your relationships, with your family, at work, and at play.

Values can drive your passion with a sense of hope, allowing you to connect with your purpose in life. Be clear about your values so that you can match what you do and the way you act to these values.

When you live by your values, you will inspire hope within yourself and others.

38.

Choose your values

Which of the following values do you want to have to improve your life and your relationships:

achievement	gentleness	money
balance	graciousness	openness
bravery	gratitude	patience
character	heart	peace
cheerfulness	helpfulness	playfulness
communication	honesty	positivity
compassion	hope	respect
confidence	humor	responsibility
courage	image	trust
creativity	intuition	truth
curiosity	inspiration	vision
direction	imagination	warmth
enrichment	kindness	well-being
friendship	listening	wisdom
fun	love	worthiness

Having clear values will guide your thoughts, words, and actions. Your unique set of values will create your future and guide you through change and difficulties.

You make hundreds of small decisions every day; your values determine the kind of decisions you make and define who you are.

39.

A worthy life

You can build a worthy life by being more resilient, and by not giving up when things go wrong. Everyone experiences difficult events and people in their lives. You build your skills through learning from these events and other people. And by being grateful for what you have learned.

When you get through hard events, you will become a more understanding, more compassionate, and wiser person. But it may not feel like this at the time.

To live a worthy life, you need to be prepared to make mistakes in order to learn. Self-belief comes from learning every day and being kind to yourself when you make mistakes.

40.

Criticism

People who criticize others without fixing or solving the problem are hard to work and live with. Don't be one of them. Be the person who fixes issues and solves problems.

When others criticize you, don't react; ask for more information and become more curious. Mostly it is not even about you; it's about them, dressed up as criticism.

When you stay calm by not reacting to criticism, you can step outside the hurt and look for what they are saying, which helps you to solve the problem, and both of you can move forward.

41.

The things you say make a difference

Change the way you speak to yourself and others to help you to focus on what is working, instead of what's not working in your life.

Use words such as *improve*, *develop*, *learn*, and *grow*. Shift away from problems toward problem-solving.

Here are some choices for changing the way you talk:

Instead of saying this:	Say this:
This is how we have failed.	*Let's learn from this.*
I can't do this; it's too hard.	*Let's just take one step at a time.*
It has to be done this way.	*Which way will serve our greater purpose?*
We can't go ahead with this.	*How can we move forward with this?*
We should have got it right.	*Let's focus on moving forward.*
We should have done something else.	*What can we do better now?*

Through your words, be the person in the room who looks for a way forward, rather than being locked in the past.

42.

Check your thoughts

You have thousands of thoughts every day. Some of them are positive, and some are negative. Many of your thoughts are influenced by other people through television, Facebook, Twitter, Instagram, and WhatsApp.

Notice your thoughts, and when you feel they are becoming more negative, speak calming words to yourself to change the direction of these negative thoughts.

Things like: *I am doing really well*, *I am doing a good job*, *I am safe*, or *I am OK*, are useful. Then take three big, long breaths after you say this to yourself.

The thoughts that come into your mind need to reflect your values.

43.

Choose your thoughts

Choosing to notice the thoughts that are not working for you is a powerful way to control negative thinking.

Say you are driving home from a friend's place late at night, and it's raining. The road is slippery, and the rain is heavy. If a thought comes into your mind of having an accident, do you think that would make you drive any more safely?

Because now your mind is seeing a car accident, this message is exactly the opposite of the one you want.

This is when you need to choose your thoughts by seeing yourself driving safely. This picture will have a more positive effect on your safety than thinking about what you don't wish to happen.

44.

Ask for help

Many people don't like to say that they have a problem or that they need help. They go through life too shy to ask for help. They don't want to appear like they are needy to others, but if they do not ask for help, they cut off the valuable tool of learning from others.

Asking for help is a way to connect to other people and to find out how they do things. We are not supposed to know everything. It's not possible. So, asking for help sometimes is the only way we can learn.

It is not a failure to ask for help; it can be a great strength. Being curious is one of the best ways we can learn and connect with others.

Chapter 6

Powerful Passion

*All our dreams can come true — if we have
the courage to pursue them.*

Walt Disney,
Founder of Disneyland.

45.

Share your passion

Was there a teacher or friend in your past who moved you with their story or their attention? They may have shared something with you that inspired you to be a better person.

Or they might have been someone who had taught the same lesson a hundred times, but their passion was as fresh and alive as if they were sharing it with you for the first time.

Be open to others, and kind with your attention and time. You never know how the small act of sharing your story might inspire another person in a small or large way.

You, too, can inspire others with your story.

46.

Be excited

Being excited is a big part of creating your passion. Excitement can be added to love, work, play, sports, music, art, and writing—to anything you do or have a passion for.

This is what you can do to connect more with your passion:

- Let yourself feel excited about life.

- Be enthusiastic.

- Trust yourself.

- Share your excitement with others.

- Believe in yourself.

- Support yourself when you make mistakes.

- Be open with others.

And when you have a small or big success, celebrate it with friends and family.

47.

Open your heart

Many people fear opening their hearts or caring for others because they think that it will be a sign of weakness, and they may not be able to control their feelings. So they close down, thinking they are keeping themselves safe.

There is always the fear that if you care for someone, you risk being hurt and that the other person may take advantage of you. Opening your heart to another person takes courage because you don't know where it may lead you.

When you choose to keep your heart open, you can fully engage with them, and it opens up the possibility of a future friendship together.

48.

Connect with others

Nothing connects us more than a shared passion or vision. We love to hear about other people's real-life stories.

When you share your stories about what excites you with the people you work and play with, it helps them to connect with you. It lets them know who you are, and what you have experienced.

Every chance you get, take the time to share your passion. This connection with others gives them the courage to tell their stories too. When you tell the stories of your past, present, and future, it helps you and others to make sense of the world.

49.

Money and passion

Many people say money is what drives their lives. They search to feel safe through having enough money, thinking that this will give them happiness. Yet money leaves many people unhappy.

Do you remember when you started your first job? Do you remember the feeling when you were first paid and saw the money in your bank account? It felt powerful. Remember walking down the street and feeling strong? And yet, lots of things and people have hurt you since that day.

Money doesn't stop anyone from being hurt.

What protects you and keeps you safe are your beliefs. You have the ability to rise above hard things when they happen, to look for how you can learn, and to move forward.

Real security is knowing that whatever happens to you in this world, you will be safe and able to work out what to do next.

Ask yourself, if money was no concern and you had all the time and money in the world, what would you do?

50.

Notice your talent

Everyone has built-in talent or talents—things that you love to do, and do with ease and joy.

When you follow your talent, you will be true to yourself, which inspires your mind, body, and soul.

Write a list of the big and little talents you have. Then write an action plan of what you will do to grow these talents. When you practice your talents every day, like playing the piano, writing, dancing, or drawing, you will get better and better at doing these things.

Many people believe that they can earn their living by using their unique talents. You deserve to do something you love.

51.

Tune into ideas

Tune into the ideas that are within your mind.

Write a list of what you would like to do, not what you *should* do, or what other people *want you* to do. Write down every idea; nothing is too big, too small, or impossible. When these ideas are joined with positive feelings, they can become a reality.

These ideas create your purpose.

Somewhere in your heart, you know what you want to do with your life. Your heart knows what it needs and wants to make your dreams come true.

Listen to your dream, visualise it, follow it, and trust it.

52.

What do you believe?

A leader was in a meeting where his team was talking about an idea they were passionate about. When they couldn't work out how to raise the money to make it happen, someone asked, "Where is the money going to come from?"

The leader replied, "Wherever it is at the moment."

Believe in yourself, your talent, and your ideas. Trust that the money for it will follow. Know that if you listen to your heart and are clear about what you want, your dreams will come true.

The more you trust your life direction, the more likely you are to draw it to you.

Chapter 7
Big Vision

*Future casting — how well we can preview
the future — is the fundamental skill for
making hope happen.*

Shane J. Lopez,
Psychologist, Scientist.

53.

A clear image

A big vision is having a clear image in your mind of what is possible for the future. Having a strong vision matters—it is more than just a goal—a vision is about your hopes and dreams. It inspires you and is a focus for your purpose and hope.

When hope is attached to vision, things that seemed hard to achieve can become easier. Having a clear vision of your future improves your health and wellness.

It's more than just being optimistic about the future; it's about creating the future you would like for yourself.

If you can hold your vision in your mind, then it has already started to happen.

54.

What is your vision?

It's easy to be caught up with everyday living—paying bills, emails, work goals, and social media. It's easy to lose sight of what motivates and excites you.

Stop for a moment and think about what's important to you, and get in touch with what you enjoy doing. Look within yourself for the hope you feel, and share your joy for your passion with others.

This becomes your vision for the future. Your vision should always stretch you a little; it needs to be something you reach for. Your vision will guide you to live a full and happy life.

55.

Positive pictures

Have you ever had your hands full of glasses, hoping that you don't drop them, and then you did? Have you been really happy in a relationship and then suddenly you stopped yourself and thought, *this can't last*, and then it didn't? Have you ever had a picture of something going wrong and held it in your mind just a little too long, and then it happened?

When these thoughts arise, as quickly as possible create a picture of what you want so that it cancels out the opposite image. It's also possible to create what you do not want by imagining it.

Remember to check that you are imagining what you want, not what you fear.

Think about your vision for today; this is how you create a positive future.

56.

Visualisation

Visualisation is the ability to create mind pictures for relaxation and for building your future. Find a safe place to lie down to read this:

Imagine you are walking in a beautiful forest after rain. The sun comes through the tall trees; you can smell the red earth, and the leaves are a deep green.

You see a river where clear water runs fast after the rain. You see the light-brown pebbles at the bottom of the river. Reaching into the river, you cup your hands to taste fresh, cold water. You feel relaxed.

Sitting on the side of the river, you feel supported by the earth. You lie back in the soft grass and close your eyes.

Imagine what it would be like to live every day filled with this beauty and joy.

Now take the time to picture your vision, imagine it clearly, and breathe into this image. Then take three deep breaths into this feeling and gently open your eyes.

This is how to visualise your future vision.

57.

Match your vision with action

The key to creating your vision is the same as the key to reaching a goal. Every day, do something big or small towards your vision. Make sure what you do most of the time supports your vision.

Prepare an A3-size picture of your vision by cutting out pictures from magazines or books of things that you want to achieve. Place this picture where you can see it every day. Feed your brain with this positive picture of your vision, as this helps you achieve it.

Big vision relies on you putting the time into seeing this every day. The magic occurs when it all comes together and the picture matches your life.

58.

Future vision

Can you remember the feeling you had after a great run, a long walk, or an enjoyable massage? When you imagine this in your mind, it creates the feelings you had when you had that experience, and your body will feel calm and relaxed.

You can create the feelings that give your body health and wellness by visualising your body in a quiet and peaceful state.

Imagine a day filled with joy and pleasure, a day filled with fun, with everything happening as you would like it to happen. Seeing a wonderful day like this in your mind creates your vision for the future and has strong health-giving powers.

Chapter 8

Inspire Intuition

*Your mind will answer most questions
if you learn to relax and
wait for the answer.*

William S. Burroughs,
Author.

59.

Use your intuition

We are all born with a strong sense of intuition — our survival depends on it.

Watch a child under seven and see how they use intuition to make decisions. They tune in to themselves and do what feels good and right for them. Intuition is the ability to know or feel something without a logical reason for feeling it. It is usually a strong physical feeling about a person or situation.

Intuition can guide you toward hope, and few emotions can bind us the way hope can. Through the darkest times in life, hope and intuition can help you to have a clear way forward.

60.

Coach intuition

We are trained from childhood to rely on logic and facts. Our schooling often tells us that there is only one right answer to a question. However, we know as adults that there are many different answers to most questions.

You need to coach your intuition to enable it to work. Meditation is a good way to connect with it; sit quietly for a short time every day, and let go of thought.

Another way to connect to intuition is to ask the world for an answer to a question. Once you have asked the question, then let go of it, and the answer will find you at the right moment.

It takes trust and self-awareness to act upon intuition.

61.

Connect to intuition

This is how you can connect to your intuition:

- Calm your mind.

- Stop your self-talk.

- Let go of any fear and worry.

- Let your thoughts come and go.

- Take several deep breaths to calm yourself.

- Close your eyes and ask yourself, "What is the best thing for me to do about this right now?"

- Sit quietly.

- Notice what you feel.

- Listen to the answers that come to you.

It will take practice to learn how to do this. As small children, this is how we managed all our decisions.

You can reconnect to your intuition again.

62.

Ah-ha moments

Everyone has had the feeling that something is not quite right, and later found that this feeling was correct.

You may have had a strong urge not to do something, only to find that the urge was right, and you were pleased you followed your intuition.

When you feel intuition, this is called an *ah-ha* moment. An idea or solution to a problem flashes into your mind. This often happens while thinking or talking about something else, and you will know the right thing to do.

Whenever or however intuition happens, it just feels right. Keep in tune with your intuition and be open to these *ah-ha* moments.

63.

Time for change

Intuition is not about being able to see into the future. It is noticing your feelings in your body, thoughts, and mind and acting on these. These feelings and thoughts will tell you when there needs to be a change in your life.

It could be time to finish a job and move on, or to change the way you think, or to change your friends, or question something that doesn't feel right to do.

If you think that something is not quite right about a person, listen to what you are feeling and act on it.

This is your intuition letting you know that something needs to change.

64.

Trust

If your intuition tells you that someone is not telling you the truth, work out if that person is doing any of these things:

- Lies about small things.
- Complains about other people who have done them wrong.
- Is unable to take responsibility for their life.
- Always blames someone else for problems and mistakes.
- Controls you in a way that doesn't feel good.
- Tries to have you to themselves, not sharing you with others.
- Speaks badly about others.
- Lets you and other people down.
- Does not do what they promise.
- Always has a good excuse for not getting things done.
- Sometimes makes the hairs on the back of your neck stand up.

If you know people who do any of these things, stay away from them because they will drain your energy. Does thinking about anything on this list set off feelings about any of your friends, family, or work colleagues?

65.

Stay calm

Staying calm is not easy when you are used to doing things all the time. Many people believe that if they are not busy, they are not of value.

Take the time to sit outside in the open air, close your eyes and relax—listen to the movement of the leaves in the trees, or the birds singing. Feel soft air on your face. Your breathing will be calmer when you notice the smells and sounds around you. This will bring you back to feeling calm.

Find those minutes; then when you feel better, walk back inside. Your mind will be calmer, and you will feel cared for by nature.

Your intuition will be always be supported by being in the natural world.

66.

Relaxation

When you are relaxed, you will find that you can connect more easily to your intuition. Try this:

- Find a quiet place to be alone.

- Close your eyes.

- Lie on the floor or a bed, or sit up with your back straight.

- Uncross your arms and legs; relax your feet.

- Take a deep breath, hold it for a couple of seconds, and then let go of that breath.

- Scan your body for any tension; then let it go.

- Drop your shoulders.

- Let your arms and legs feel heavy.

Now visualise the way you would like an event or a situation to be in the future, with lots of detail. At the right time your intuition will kick in, and you will know what to do next.

Chapter 9
Take Risks

If you don't like something, change it.
If you can't change it, change your attitude.

Maya Angelou,
Author, Activist.

67.

Risk to change

Many things can stop you from taking risks. For example, you may feel that you need to find out all the information about something before you decide.

It's not possible to find out everything.

Technology moves so quickly that even if you were to put together all the information needed to decide, by the time you did that, new information would have come to light.

Everything you've seen, heard, and felt, is recorded in your mind—trust it, listen to it, feel it, and act upon it.

At some point, you need to act—so trust what you know now and take more risks.

68.

Your path

Listening to what other people think can stop you from taking risks. If you want to do something new, friends or work colleagues may tell you that what you're doing is not possible. Especially if you want to do something new or different.

They may say, "You can't do that, it will never work," or "You won't have enough money to do that," or "It's been done before, and it didn't work."

Sure, it may have been done before, but the timing is different now. It may be that people weren't ready for it before and could be ready now.

Everything your mind can dream about can be achieved. Be prepared to take a risk, to achieve in a new way.

Learn to follow your own path and take the risks that feel right for you.

69.

Change is constant

Whether change is big, such as moving house or a divorce—or something small, like the bus you catch to work goes a different way, your reply is not usually, "Great I love change!" It is more likely to be, "Why is this happening to me?"

Change is hard for everyone unless you have been part of the decision to change.

As the world changes, we must change too—the way we talk to each other, the way we connect, the way we manage people, and the way we look to the future.

Just as we expect the latest phone to be easier to use, do more than the one before, and take better photos, we must ask ourselves to be more open to new ideas.

Life is filled with new ideas. But you need to let go of old ideas to make room for new ones to enter.

70.

Risk thinking

Here are some of the things you can do to change your thinking about risk.

- Stay connected to your vision and keep planning and talking about it.

- Keep believing in your ideas; go for what you really want.

- Take small steps; do something toward your idea every day.

- Let go of the past, and see taking a risk as a way for you to grow.

- Learn new ways of doing things.

- Every day, do something you are afraid of—or something hard to do.

- Other people may try to talk you out of taking a risk. Don't listen to them.

- Keep going.

If you have an idea that excites you, take the risk of trying it. You will never know if it works unless you try.

71.

Follow through

Very often, people with big ideas don't check the progress of their idea or take responsibility for how and when goals are reached. To follow through with your idea is as important as having the idea in the first place.

The actor Michelle Pfeiffer quotes her father's words to her, "Trust everyone, but cut the cards." This means you will have to trust people to help you with your idea, but you need to make sure that you check its progress. Make sure that everyone knows what they are meant to be doing with the idea and what they need to do next.

When the risk finds its purpose, it is worth it.

72.

Tools for risk-taking

Fear is the one thing that stops you from taking risks. There is fear of what may happen, and fear of being wrong. But if you don't take risks, you will never know what you could have achieved.

Here are some ideas to overcome the fear of taking a risk:

- Don't wait for all the information before you start with your idea.

- Be willing to learn new things.

- Play with ideas that come to you.

- Don't expect that everyone will like your idea.

- Trust yourself.

- Create a safe place where it's OK to discuss your ideas.

- Don't be put off by the negatives from others.

- Learn from mistakes and move forward.

- Follow through.

- Be gentle with yourself if you make mistakes.

Mistakes are part of risk-taking; they are how you learn.

73.

Creative thinking

A group of new nurses was asked on their first day, "Why do doctors need to wear masks while they are operating?" Back came the reply, "Well, if they make a mistake, no one will know who did it." Everyone laughed because the answer was not expected.

Wouldn't it be wonderful if you could take the risk-taking from your childhood into your adult life? If you could see every color and shape with the same clear, open eyes?

When you took your first step as a baby, you took a chance because you wanted to. Try bringing back some of that childlike wonder to look at the world with wide baby eyes again.

Listen for the ideas that, when linked with what you are doing, become the right risks to take now.

Chapter 10
Compassion

*Compassion and tolerance are not a sign of
weakness, but a sign of strength.*

Dalai Lama,
Spiritual Leader of Tibet.

74.

Compassion brings us together

Compassion means treating yourself and others with respect, forgiveness, empathy, and kindness. It's not about fixing others. Your job is to fix you, and their job is to fix themselves.

The old way of being cold at work and kind in your personal life is not sustainable. Many people are tired of their uncaring lives and want to be more compassionate.

We are more likely to feel compassion for others if we have had hard times or been hurt. Compassion goes straight to the heart and opens it. On that level, everyone is equal.

When we respond with compassion about sad events, this deep level of compassion brings us together. We seek compassion because, with all the change and pain in the world, without it, we would be heartbroken.

75.

Think globally, act locally

Compassion keeps you from going into the fight, flight, or freeze reaction.

Fight, flight, and freeze work like this: you may want to *fight* or argue with another person because they hurt you. You may want to take *flight*, or run away and hide, because another person has hurt you. You may want to *freeze*, which is doing nothing, because another person hurt you. None of these things will help you to move forward.

Compassion is the way to move forward—both for yourself and the other person.

In every step you take, being compassionate means breathing deeply, speaking and thinking kindly about yourself and others, and giving other people the benefit of the doubt.

76.

Stay with the discomfort

Allowing yourself to feel sad or unhappy when something wrong or bad happens is the first step to facing problems. The more discomfort you feel, the more important it is to deal with this problem.

When you work through problems, you become a stronger person and grow your level of compassion.

Think about what you can do differently next time, and write it in your diary. This is a positive way to feel your feelings and move forward.

Bringing compassion into your personal and work lives will allow your whole self to be present, not just the image that you like to show to the outside world.

Be brave, more open, and compassionate with yourself and others.

77.

Body language

Other people's body language will tell you if they are stressed or worried, or whether they care about what they are hearing or seeing.

Being a compassionate person will help you to notice what other people are feeling, which includes reading their body language. Seventy-five percent of the message that is sent or received is in their body language. Watch carefully what they are doing to read their body language.

When people feel understood, they are more likely to want to listen to you.

When you first listen to understand them, it can be easier for them to understand and be compassionate with you.

78.

It could have been you

It is easy to watch someone do something wrong and then be unkind or mean to them about it.

The truth is that it could have been you who did that wrong thing—everyone makes mistakes. In that, we are all equal in life.

Being compassionate is being kind to someone who has made a mistake, not being hurtful or mean.

Look for ways to connect with them rather than telling them what they have done wrong, which only adds to how badly they feel. Treat them the way you would like to be treated, had it been you who made the mistake.

79.

Connect with compassion

When you become a more compassionate person, you are more open to other people and are able to connect to them. Here are some steps you can take to be a more compassionate person:

- Forgive someone who it is hard for you to forgive.

- Forgive yourself for the part you played in things that have hurt you in the past.

- Listen to others and connect with them.

- Talk kindly with other people.

- Lighten up, and have a sense of humor.

- Be gentle on yourself.

- Treat other people with respect; most people are doing their best.

Remember you are enough, you have enough, and you do enough. Accept that you can improve but that you are a good person.

80.

Forgive quickly

One of the biggest choices we have is how and when to forgive. Everyone can forgive, but it's not always easy.

Time does heal all wounds, but forgiving heals them in the moment we forgive.

Many people have long-held bad feelings about people or events, past or present. They may be unhappy about not having enough schooling, or worry that it was not a good enough education. They may not have had enough love in the past. Many things can be the reason for past sadness.

You wouldn't be human unless you had some sadness from the past.

The key is to learn from this. Stop looking at what went wrong, accept what happened, and forgive whatever hurt you in the past.

He who forgives ends the quarrel.
—African proverb.

81.

It's not personal

When someone says or does something hurtful, or something you don't agree with, this is when you need to love and nurture yourself the most.

Be gentle and kind in your self-talk, and imagine opening your heart to yourself.

Ask yourself, "If the opposite were true, would this change the way I see this problem?" Let yourself see both sides of the issue. When you turn the thought around, it becomes less personal.

Focus on how you can nurture your thoughts and feelings and forgive the other person.

82.

Starts and finishes

Life is about starts and finishes. Nothing ever stays the same.

It is up to you to find out how you can learn to love, let go, forgive others, leave the past behind, live in the present, and be a part of the future.

If you get stuck in the same sadness as last year or the year before by feeling hate, guilt, or jealousy, this will hold you back. You won't be able to set clear goals for the future.

Today is a new beginning. Make some new goals for how you want your future to be and try to act in a way that supports your goal. You hold your future in your own hands, based on the way you think and feel. It's up to you to bring compassion and kindness into your life.

Chapter 11
Connection

*I define connection as the energy that exists
between people when they feel seen,
heard, and valued; when they can give and
receive without judgment;
and when they derive sustenance and
strength from the relationship.*

Brené Brown,
Speaker, Author.

83.

Deep connection

A hope-filled life means connecting to others in a deeper, more real way.

When our needs for food, water, warmth, and rest are met, we next require safety, and then we want relationships and friendships. Connection with others is the way to build these.

Be honest and open in the way you speak with others, and focus on what's happening now. If you are always thinking about the past, it's going to be hard to connect with other people in the present.

Deep connection is when you focus on who you are with and what they are saying as if they are the most important person in the world. Make this your one important goal for connection—speak and listen with all your attention to whomever you are with.

84.

Healthy connection

Everyone wants love, support, and friendship—your need to belong is very strong. Your need to be seen and understood is part of your need for connection, to be known for who or what you are, to be noticed.

Connection to others is one of the best ways to keep yourself healthy and well. Whether it's a relationship with family, work colleagues, friends, or your partner, getting along with other people is one of life's biggest needs.

Connect—don't cut yourself off from family and friends, as this will only cause sadness.

Show interest in other people—ask them about their lives, and listen carefully to their answers. Be willing to be deeply connected with others.

85.

Focus on what's working

When you think too much about the things that have gone wrong in your life, it is easy to become disconnected from others. If you speak mostly about all the negatives, you will believe you are a negative person.

The things that have gone wrong are only a small part of any day, probably less than twenty percent of what you have done on that day. Think also about the other eighty percent that went well.

Make sure you talk positively about what has worked well in your life. You will feel happier, and the world will seem a much better place.

Catch yourself and others doing things right, and tell them.

86.

Journaling

Writing in a journal or a notebook about what you are grateful for makes your life more joyful and positive. You could also use your phone as your journal.

This can take you five to fifteen minutes each morning or evening.

Every day, write three sentences about what you are happy about in your life. Things like: *I am grateful for this happy day, I am grateful to have work, I am grateful to have kind friends, I am grateful for the sun shining,* or *I am grateful that I am strong and happy.*

Writing about what brings you joy brings these things into the light, where you can see them more clearly.

Journaling is a healthy way to talk about your feelings on paper. By looking at your journal, you can see your progress over time.

87.

Stop being so nice

Most of us were taught to be nice, to always smile, no matter what is happening in our life.

Being nice might please someone else but often means that you let yourself down. People keep any anger they feel hidden so that they appear to have their lives in control.

But being nice at the cost of hiding your real thoughts and feelings doesn't serve you well.

You need to let people know when you are hurt, and stop hiding your feelings. Speak to others more honestly so that you can connect to them, and then let the feelings go.

It may be uncomfortable at first, but try doing this often. The more you try, the better you will become at being your true self.

88.

The gift of self-love

Most people were never shown how to like or love themselves.

Learn to be kind to yourself by deciding to like yourself more; accept who you are, and speak kind words to yourself. This will bring more hope into your world and help you to be more self-loving.

Take the time to slow down. Calm yourself by taking deep breaths and by noticing what is happening in the present moment. Try meditation, yoga, walking, or exercise. All of these things will care for you and help you to learn to love yourself more. When you do this, you become more confident and caring.

Repeat this to yourself often: *I have all the time in the world to be kind and self-loving to myself.*

Self-love is a gift of kindness that you give to yourself.

89.

Listen more than you speak

Sometimes when you feel insecure around other people, you may want to fill the quiet spaces with over-talking. Could you be quieter, rather than filling this space with words?

Even when you are asked for advice, listen more than you speak. Let the other person find their own answers by listening to themselves while they speak.

When someone talks about their problems out loud, they will often see and hear these problems differently. Ask open questions like, "Can you tell me more about that?" or "What do you think?" This allows others to solve their problems themselves.

Listening builds trust; telling other people what to think, feel or do, doesn't build trust.

Chapter 12
Committed Tribes

*Call it a clan, call it a network,
call it a tribe, call it a family.
Whatever you call it, whoever you are,
you need one.*

Jane Howard,
Journalist.

90.

Share hope

Everyone wants to be inspired; everyone wants to be a part of something bigger than they are. Hope is something you can share with your family.

Talk with your family to decide what you value as a family, just as you would at work. Give everyone a say about what they value, from the youngest to the oldest.

If these values are about being gentle, kind, and respecting others, write them in a place where the whole family can see them, on a wall or noticeboard.

These values will offer a sense of security within your family as you are all working toward the same values.

91.

Daily values

Talk about your values often, and bring them to life in everyday living.

When your family meets together at the end of the day, ask each other for an example of how you used your family values at school or work. A child could speak of how one of their friends was bullied at school and how she sat with them afterwards, and gently told them things would be OK.

An adult may tell the family about how she listened well in a meeting at work and how she showed respect to the team by doing this.

Sharing a clear set of values as a family can extend hope in your family and to the world.

92.

Build trust

Children and teenagers often say they don't feel heard in their family, that their parents spend most of their time telling them about their mistakes and not their strengths. That they are too busy to listen to them.

To develop trust in families, we need to listen to each other more. Everyone loves to be heard, to be listened to carefully.

Being open with another person will show that you care about what they say, even if you don't agree.

Make your goal with your family to be a good listener. This helps the whole family to be better people.

93.

Are you controlling?

Do you help other people to solve problems, or do you solve them for them? Do you let others learn from mistakes, or do you try to stop them from feeling any pain?

A caring adult makes sure their children are safe but allows them to learn from their mistakes. Let go of the need to control by teaching your children how to catch a train or a bus, cook at least one meal, use the washing machine, sew a button and hem a skirt or pants, walk tall and safely at night, and care for others.

These skills will nurture them through life and do more for their self-esteem than any amount of protecting them will.

94.

Choose what to watch

Many people don't feel safe because they watch screens too much. They see a view of what is happening in the world that shows negative messages most of the time.

Things look bigger and more unsafe on a screen, and young people don't always know how to make sense of world events, so they become scared.

Don't complain about how the media makes things bigger than they are; the way to deal with it is to turn the screens off for a while every day, and limit time on your phones.

You will feel a lot safer if the bad news of the world is not shown all the time.

95.

Hold the vision

One of the most powerful things you can do as a family is to hold a hopeful vision of the future, no matter what is happening in your world right now.

Children will grow into kind, loving adults if they have a clear picture of your family as healthy, well-balanced people in the world, whatever their talents and abilities are at the moment.

Close your eyes now and see your family in ten years as healthy, well-balanced, kind people. Experience how it feels to think of your family in this way. Doing this often helps you as a family to become that positive vision of the future.

96.

Learning is the goal

It is hard sometimes to ask children, especially teen-agers, to do their jobs around the house. When their beds aren't made, or the lights are left on, or their rooms are untidy, try to look at what your children are doing well.

Many children feel that their parents look for mistakes instead of what they are doing right. If all that children see and hear about is their mistakes, they will think they are a mistake.

Show your child how they can get better so they can learn.

Remember to use lots of positive words.

Children might pretend not to care, but they do. By noticing the positives things that they do, and telling them about it, children learn what you expect from them about it, and that will last forever.

97.

Your example

The best way to teach good values to your family is by living them yourself.

It doesn't work if you tell someone to do something, and then do it another way yourself. What you do shows others what you expect them to do much more than what you say.

If you want to be trusted, be more supportive. If you inspire trust in others, they will find a way to live up to it.

If you want to be respected, be more respectful. This includes saying, "Please," and "Thank you," and following the values you have set.

Respect in families builds feelings of trust, safety, and well-being.

98.

Support each other

Constantly finding things that are wrong in your family will not create a happy, healthy family.

Use words that are kind and clear, like: *Please do this*, *Thank you for doing that*, *I look forward to seeing you soon*, or *Thank you for waiting for me*. The more you use positive words, the more you build your relationships with others in your family. Positive words create strong bonds.

A loving person will notice and support others when they are getting things nearly right. Noticing others doing the right thing often builds confident and loving families.

99.

Natural leaders

Let your children choose the values they want for the family. Children are natural leaders. You only have to look at how they negotiate for pizza on a Friday night to see this. Help them to develop these skills.

Give your children new things to do, and trust them to do their best. Allow your children to lead you sometimes. Believe in them to show you the way sometimes.

You don't need to scare children into doing what you have asked them to do; you need to care for them, and, by your example, show them how to live with trust and compassion.

Loving parents know that they and their children have separate lives and are happy to focus on their own lives while supporting their children in theirs. Children don't become perfect; they just get better with love and guidance.

100.

Being a better person

Many parents measure themselves through their work goals and how much money they make. It can be difficult to put the same energy and value into raising children because the results are harder to measure and the task often seems thankless.

This doesn't mean you shouldn't try to be a better person and a better parent.

The same leadership skills used to lead a team or a business can be used in your family. No matter how old you or your children are, you can still learn to be more loving, more supportive, more caring, and a more open person in your family.

You can be a better leader with your children now, whatever age they are.

Postscript

There are many ideas in this book about the ways you can access hope to create a happier, and more enjoyable future—where your dreams can come true. I have shared with you the tools I have developed as a result of my life experience.

Hope doesn't stop challenging things from happening in life, it just helps you to understand that they are transitory. Through applying life skills, you can learn, grow and move forward with greater strength and personal power.

I am a hopeful person because, in spite of all life's challenges, I am passionate about living an examined life, and planet earth is a magnificent place to learn to be your very best self.

As a small child, I remember the excitement of saying goodbye to my favorite aunt as she boarded a luxury liner from Sydney Harbour, heading to Southampton. She threw a yellow streamer from the upper deck, which I eagerly caught on the dock below, and held on to it tightly, smiling and waving with my other hand. This left an indelible mark on my imagination. Now as an adult, hope for me is the streamer between the ocean liner and the dock. Between me and my future.

I hope this book is like that streamer, a link that can connect you to hope for your future.

Word List

・本文で使われている全ての語を掲載しています（LEVEL 1、2）。ただし、LEVEL 3以上は、中学校レベルの語を含みません。

・語形が規則変化する語の見出しは原形で示しています。不規則変化語は本文中で使われている形になっています。

・一般的な意味を紹介していますので、一部の語で本文で実際に使われている品詞や意味と合っていないことがあります。

・品詞は以下のように示しています。

图 名詞	代 代名詞	形 形容詞	副 副詞	動 動詞	助 助動詞
前 前置詞	接 接続詞	間 間投詞	冠 冠詞	略 略語	俗 俗語
頭 接頭語	尾 接尾語	記 記号	関 関係代名詞		

A

□ **A3-size** A3（用紙）サイズの

□ **ability** 图 ①できること，（～する）能力 ②才能

□ **about** 前 care about ～を気にかける hear about ～について聞く worried about《be –》（～のことで）心配している，～が気になる［かかる］ worry about ～のことを心配する

□ **accept** 動 ①受け入れる ②同意する，認める

□ **access** 图 ①接近，近づく方法，通路 ②（システムなどへの）アクセス 動 アクセスする

□ **accident** 图 ①（不慮の）事故，災難 ②偶然

□ **achieve** 動 成し遂げる，達成する，成功を収める

□ **achievement** 图 ①達成，成就 ②業績

□ **act** 图 行為，行い 動 ①行動する ②機能する ③演じる

□ **activated** 形 ①活性化した ②作動された

□ **actively** 副 活発に，活動的に

□ **activist** 图 活動家，実践主義者

□ **actor** 图 俳優，役者

□ **add** 動 ①加える，足す ②足し算をする ③言い添える

□ **adult** 图 大人，成人 形 大人の，成人した

□ **advantage** 图 有利な点［立場］，強み，優越 take advantage of ～を利用する，～につけ込む

□ **adventure** 图 冒険 動 危険をおかす

□ **advice** 图 忠告，助言，意見

□ **affect** 動 ①影響する ②（病気などが）おかす ③ふりをする 图 感情，欲望

□ **affirmation** 图 ①断言，確約 ②肯定命題［判断］

□ **afraid of**《be –》～を恐れる，～を怖がる

□ **African** 形 アフリカ（人）の 图 アフリカ人

□ **after** 熟 come after ～のあとを追う look after ～の世話をする，～に気をつける

□ **afterwards** 副 その後，のちに

□ **agent** 图 ①代理人 ②代表者

□ **agree with**（人）に同意する

□ **ah-ha** 間 ①〔理解できたとき〕分かった，なるほど，そうか ②〔驚き・喜

130

び・発見の気持ち〕ははあ, へえ！

- [ ] **ahead** 熟 go ahead with〔計画・仕事などを〕進める

- [ ] **aim** 動①（武器・カメラなどを）向ける ②ねらう, 目指す 名ねらい, 目標

- [ ] **air** 熟 open air 戸外, 野外

- [ ] **alarm** 名①警報, 目覚まし時計 ②驚き, 突然の恐怖 動①はっとさせる ②警報を発する

- [ ] **Alexandria** 名アレクサンドリア《エジプトの地名》

- [ ] **all** 熟 all over the world 世界中に all the time いつも, その間ずっと not at all 少しも～でない with all ～がありながら, あらゆる～をこめて

- [ ] **allow** 動①許す,《 – … to ～》…が～するのを可能にする, …に～させておく ②与える

- [ ] **along** 熟 get along with（人）と仲良くする, 歩調を合わせる

- [ ] **although** 接 ～だけれども, ～にもかかわらず, たとえ～でも

- [ ] **always** 熟 not always 必ずしも～であるとは限らない

- [ ] **amount** 名①量, 額 ②《the – 》合計 動（総計～に）なる

- [ ] **and** 熟 and yet それなのに, それにもかかわらず between A and B A とBの間に both A and B A もB も come and go 行き来する, 現れては消える

- [ ] **angel** 名①天使 ②天使のような人

- [ ] **anger** 名怒り 動怒る, ～を怒らせる

- [ ] **antidote** 名①解毒剤 ②防御手段, 対抗手段

- [ ] **anxiety** 名①心配, 不安 ②切望

- [ ] **anxious** 形①心配な, 不安な ②切望して

- [ ] **any** 熟 at any moment 今すぐにも

- [ ] **anyone** 代①《疑問文・条件節で》誰か《否定文で》誰も（～ない）③《肯定文で》誰でも

- [ ] **appear** 動①現れる, 見えてくる ②（～のように）見える, ～らしい appear to するように見える

- [ ] **apply** 動①申し込む, 志願する ②あてはまる ③適用する

- [ ] **approval** 名①賛成 ②承認, 認可

- [ ] **argue** 動①論じる, 議論する ②主張する

- [ ] **arise** 動①起こる, 生じる ②起きる, 行動を開始する ③（死から）よみがえる ④（風が）たつ

- [ ] **around** 熟 rush around trying to ～で走り回る, ～に急ぐ turn around 向きを変える, 方向転換する

- [ ] **artist** 名芸術家

- [ ] **as** 熟 as a result of ～の結果（として）as if あたかも～のように, まるで～みたいに as soon as ～するとすぐ, ～するや否や as well その上, 同様に as well as ～と同様に as～as possible できるだけ～ just as（ちょうど）であろうとおり see ～ as … ～を…と考える such as たとえば～, ～のような the same～as […that]…～と同じ（ような）～

- [ ] **ask ～ if** ～かどうか尋ねる

- [ ] **ask for help** 助けを頼む

- [ ] **assist** 動手伝う, 列席する, 援助する

- [ ] **assumption** 名前提, 想定, 仮定

- [ ] **at** 熟 at a time 一度に, 続けざまに at any moment 今すぐにも at first 最初は, 初めのうちは at home 自宅で, くつろいで at least 少なくとも at the end of ～の終わりに at the moment 今は at the time そのころ, 当時は at work 働いて, 仕事中で not at all 少しも～でない

- [ ] **attach** 動①取り付ける, 添える ②付随する, 帰属する

- [ ] **attached** 動 attach（取りつける）の過去, 過去分詞 形ついている, 結びついた,《be - to ～》～に未練［愛着］がある

A
B
C
D
E
F
G
H
I
J
K
L
M
N
O
P
Q
R
S
T
U
V
W
X
Y
Z

131

□ **attention** 名 ①注意, 集中 ②配慮, 手当て, 世話 **pay attention to** 〜に注意を払う 間《号令として》気をつけ

□ **attitude** 名 姿勢, 態度, 心構え

□ **Australia** 名 オーストラリア《国名》

□ **author** 名 著者, 作家 動 著作する, 創作する

□ **average** 名 平均(値), 並み **on (the) average** 平均して 形 平均の, 普通の 動 平均して〜になる

□ **aware** 形 ①気がついて, 知って ②(〜の)認識のある **aware of**《be 〜》〜に気がついている

□ **awareness** 名 認識, 自覚, 意識性, 気づいていること

□ **away** 熟 **move away from** 〜から遠ざかる **run away** 走り去る, 逃げ出す **stay away from** 〜から離れている

B

□ **back** 熟 **bring back** 戻す, 呼び戻す **get back** 戻る, 帰る

□ **badly** 副 ①悪く, まずく, へたに ②とても, ひどく

□ **balance** 名 ①均衡, 平均, 落ち着き ②てんびん ③残高, 差額 動 釣り合いをとる

□ **bank account** 銀行預金口座

□ **base** 名 基礎, 土台, 本部 動《 – on 〜》〜に基礎を置く, 基づく

□ **battle** 名 戦闘, 戦い 動 戦う

□ **beauty** 名 ①美, 美しい人[物] ②《the – 》美点

□ **bed** 熟 **get out of bed** 起きる, 寝床を離れる

□ **begin with** 〜で始まる, 〜から始める

□ **beginning** 動 begin (始まる) の現在分詞 名 初め, 始まり

□ **behavior** 名 振る舞い, 態度, 行動

□ **behind** 前 ①〜の後ろに, 〜の背後に ②〜に遅れて, 〜に劣って 副 ①後ろに, 背後に ②遅れて, 劣って **leave behind** あとにする, 〜を置き去りにする

□ **being** 動 be (〜である) の現在分詞 名 存在, 生命, 人間

□ **belief** 名 信じること, 信念, 信用

□ **believe in** 〜を信じる

□ **believing** 形 信じる 名 信じること

□ **belong** 動《 – to 〜》〜に属する, 〜のものである

□ **below** 前 ①〜より下に ②〜以下の, 〜より劣る 副 下に[へ]

□ **benefit** 名 ①利益, 恩恵 ②(失業保険・年金などの)手当, 給付(金) 動 利益を得る, (〜の)ためになる

□ **beside** 前 ①〜のそばに, 〜と並んで ②〜と比べると ③〜とはずれて

□ **besides** 前 ①〜に加えて, 〜のほかに ②《否定文・疑問文で》〜を除いて 副 その上, さらに

□ **best** 熟 **do one's best** 全力を尽くす

□ **better** 熟 **feel better** 気分がよくなる **get better** 良くなる, 上達する

□ **between A and B** AとBの間に

□ **bill** 名 ①請求書, 勘定書 ②法案 ③紙幣 ④ビラ ⑤くちばし 動 ①請求書を送る ②勘定書に記入する

□ **bind** 動 ①縛る, 結ぶ ②束縛する, 義務づける

□ **bit** 動 bite (かむ) の過去, 過去分詞 名 ①小片, 少量 ②《a – 》少し, ちょっと ③(情報量単位の)ビット

□ **blame** 動 とがめる, 非難する 名 ①責任, 罪 ②非難

□ **board** 名 ①板, 掲示板 ②委員会, 重役会 動 ①乗り込む ②下宿する

□ **bond** 名 結びつき，結束 動 結束する［させる］，結合する

□ **both A and B** AもBも

□ **bottom** 名 ①底，下部，すそ野，ふもと，最下位，根底 ②尻 形 底の，根底の

□ **bounce** 動 ①弾む，跳ね上がる ②弾ませる，跳ね返す 名 弾み，弾力性

□ **brain** 名 ①脳 ②知力

□ **brave** 形 勇敢な 動 勇敢に立ち向かう

□ **bravery** 名 勇敢さ，勇気ある行動

□ **break** 熟 take a break 休息する

□ **breath** 名 ①息，呼吸 ②《a-》（風の）そよぎ，気配，きざし，**take a deep breath in** 息を深く吸う

□ **breathe** 動 ①呼吸する ②ひと息つく，休息する

□ **breathing** 動 breathe（呼吸する）の現在分詞 名 ①呼吸，息づかい ②《a-》ひと息の間，ちょっとの間

□ **brilliant** 形 光り輝く，見事な，すばらしい

□ **bring back** 戻す，呼び戻す

□ **build on** 〜の上に築く，〜を基にして前進する

□ **building** 動 build（建てる）の現在分詞 名 建物，建造物，ビルディング

□ **built-in** 形 ①組み込みの，内蔵の ②生来の，固有の，本質的な

□ **bully** 動 いじめる，おどす 名 いじめっ子

□ **but** 熟 not 〜 but … 〜ではなくて…

□ **by nature** 生まれつき

□ **by the time** 〜する時までに

□ **by way of** 〜を手段として，〜のために

C

□ **call someone to** （人）に呼びかける，声をかける

□ **calm** 形 穏やかな，落ち着いた 名 静けさ，落ち着き 動 静まる，静める

□ **Can you 〜?** 〜してくれますか。

□ **cancel** 動 取り消し，使用中止 動 取り消す，中止する

□ **care about** 〜を気にかける

□ **care for** 〜の世話をする，〜を大事に思う

□ **career** 名 ①（生涯の・専門的な）職業 ②経歴，キャリア

□ **caring** 形 世話をする，面倒を見る，気遣う 名 介護，思いやり，世話，福祉活動，優しさ

□ **casting** 名 ①投げること ②〔視線を〕投じること ③配役，割当

□ **caught up with** 《be-》〜にとらわれる，〜のとりこになる

□ **celebrate** 動 ①祝う，祝福する ②祝典を開く

□ **challenge** 名 ①挑戦 ②難関 動 挑む，試す

□ **challenging** 動 challenge（挑戦する）の現在分詞 形 能力が試される，やる気をそそる

□ **chance** 熟 take a chance 一か八かやってみる

□ **chapter** 名 （書物の）章

□ **character** 名 ①特性，個性 ②（小説・劇などの）登場人物 ③文字，記号 ④品性，人格

□ **check** 動 ①照合する，検査する ②阻止［妨害］する ③（所持品を）預ける 名 ①照合，検査 ②小切手 ③（突然の）停止，阻止（するもの）④伝票，勘定書

□ **cheerful** 形 上機嫌の，元気のよい，（人を）気持ちよくさせる

□ **cheerfulness** 名 上機嫌

□ **childhood** 名 幼年［子ども］時代

□ **childlike** 形子どもらしい

□ **choice** 图①選択(の範囲・自由), え
り好み, 選ばれた人[物] 形精選した

□ **circle** 图①円, 円周, 輪 ②循環, 軌
道 ③仲間, サークル 動回る, 囲む

□ **clan** 图①氏族 ②一家, 一門

□ **clarify** 動①明確にする, 解明する
②浄化する

□ **clear** 形①はっきりした, 明白な
②澄んだ ③(よく)晴れた 動①は
っきりさせる ②片づける ③晴れる
副①はっきりと ②すっかり, 完全に

□ **clearly** 副①明らかに, はっきりと
②《返答に用いて》そのとおり

□ **client** 图依頼人, 顧客, クライアン
ト

□ **co-produce** 動共同で生産[製造・
制作]する

□ **coach** 图①長距離用のバス ②(鉄
道の)普通客車 ③大型四輪馬車 ④コ
ーチ, 指導者

□ **colleague** 图同僚, 仲間, 同業者

□ **come** 熟 come after ～のあとを追
う come and go 行き来する, 現れ
ては消える come into one's mind
(人)の心に浮かんでくる come
through 通り抜ける come true 実
現する

□ **commit** 動①委託する ②引き受
ける ③(罪などを)犯す

□ **committed** 形①〔主義や行動な
どに〕傾倒した, 情熱を注いだ ②〔お
互いに〕信頼し合った, 献身的な ③
〔立場や考えを〕はっきり表明した

□ **communicate** 動①連絡する,
通信する ②伝える, 明らかにする

□ **communication** 图伝えること,
伝導, 連絡

□ **compassion** 图思いやり, 深い同
情

□ **compassionate** 形思いやりの
ある, 慈悲深い, 心の優しい

□ **complain** 動①不平[苦情]を言う,

ぶつぶつ言う ②(病状などを)訴え
る

□ **complete** 形完全な, まったくの,
完成した 動完成させる

□ **concern** 動①関係する, 《be -ed
in [with] ～》～に関係している ②心
配させる, 《be -ed about [for] ～》～
を心配する 图①関心事 ②関心, 心
配 ③関係, 重要性

□ **confidence** 图自信, 確信, 信頼,
信用度

□ **confident** 形自信のある, 自信に
満ちた

□ **connect** 動つながる, つなぐ, 関
係づける

□ **connected** 動 connect(つながる)
の過去, 過去分詞 形結合した, 関係
のある

□ **connection** 图①つながり, 関係
②縁故

□ **constant** 形①絶えない, 一定の,
不変の ②不屈の, 確固たる 图定数

□ **constantly** 副絶えず, いつも, 絶
え間なく

□ **contribute** 動①貢献する ②寄
稿する ③寄付する

□ **control** 動①管理[支配]する ②
抑制する, コントロールする 图①管
理, 支配(力) ②抑制 in control ～
を支配して, ～を掌握している

□ **conversation** 图会話, 会談

□ **corporate** 形団体[共同]の, 会社
の

□ **correct** 形正しい, 適切な, りっぱ
な 動(誤りを)訂正する, 直す

□ **cost** 图①値段, 費用 ②損失, 犠牲
動(金・費用が)かかる, (～を)要する,
(人に金額を)費やさせる

□ **could** 熟 could have done ～だっ
たかもしれない《仮定法》Could you
～? ～してくださいますか。If +《主
語》+ could ～できればなあ《仮定法》

□ **counseling** 图カウンセリング,
相談, 助言

□ **count** 動①数える ②(〜を…と)みなす ③重要[大切]である 名計算, 総計, 勘定

□ **couple** 名①2つ, 対 ②夫婦, 一組 ③数個 couple of《a –》2, 3の 動つなぐ, つながる, 関連させる

□ **courage** 名勇気, 度胸

□ **crazy** 形①狂気の, ばかげた, 無茶な ②夢中の, 熱狂的な

□ **create** 動創造する, 生み出す, 引き起こす

□ **creative** 形創造力のある, 独創的な

□ **creativity** 名創造性, 独創力

□ **credit** 名①信用, 評判, 名声 ②掛け売り, 信用貸し 動信用する

□ **criticism** 名批評, 非難, 反論, 評論

□ **criticize** 動批判[批評]する, 評論する

□ **curiosity** 名①好奇心 ②珍しい物[存在]

□ **curious** 形好奇心の強い, 珍しい, 奇妙な, 知りたがる

□ **cut off** 切断する, 切り離す

□ **cut out** 切り取る, 切り抜く

□ **cut someone off from** (人)を〜から切り離す

□ **cutting** 動cut (切る)の現在分詞 名①切ること, 裁断, カッティング ②(新聞などの)切り抜き, (挿し木用の)切り枝

□ **cycle** 名周期, 循環 動循環する

D

□ **daily** 形毎日の, 日常の 副毎日, 日ごとに 名《-lies》日刊新聞

□ **dancing** 動dance (踊る)の現在分詞 名ダンス, 舞踏

□ **day** 熟every day 毎日

□ **deal** 動①分配する ②《 – with [in] 〜》〜を扱う 名①取引, 扱い ②(不特定の)量, 額 a good [great] deal (of 〜) かなり[ずいぶん・大量](の〜), 多額(の〜)

□ **decade** 名10年間

□ **decide to do** 〜することに決める

□ **decision** 名①決定, 決心 ②判決

□ **deck** 名(船の)デッキ, 甲板, 階, 床

□ **deep** 熟take a deep breath in 息を深く吸う

□ **deep-diaphragm** 形横隔膜の深く, 深い腹式の

□ **deeply** 副深く, 非常に

□ **define** 動①定義する, 限定する ②〜の顕著な特性である

□ **depend** 動《 – on [upon] 〜》①〜を頼る, 〜をあてにする ②〜による, 〜次第である

□ **depression** 名①不景気, 不況 ②憂うつ, 意気消沈

□ **derive** 動①由来する, 派生する ②(本源から)引き出す ③由来をたどる

□ **deserve** 動(〜を)受けるに足る, 値する, (〜して)当然である

□ **detail** 名①細部, 《-s》詳細 ②《-s》個人情報 動詳しく述べる

□ **determine** 動①決心する[させる] ②決定する[させる] ③測定する

□ **develop** 動①発達する[させる] ②開発する

□ **development** 名①発達, 発展 ②開発

□ **diary** 名日記

□ **differently** 副(〜と)異なって, 違って

□ **difficulty** 名①難しいこと, 難題 ②大変な努力, 労力 ③困窮, 窮乏

□ **dignity** 名威厳, 品位, 尊さ, 敬意

□ **direct** 形まっすぐな, 直接の, 率

直な, 露骨な 副 まっすぐに, 直接に 動 ①指導する, 監督する ②(目・注意・努力などを)向ける

□ **direction** 名①方向, 方角 ②《-s》指示, 説明書 ③指導, 指揮

□ **disappear** 動見えなくなる, 姿を消す, なくなる

□ **discomfort** 名不快(なこと), 辛苦, つらさ

□ **disconnected** 形①切断[分離]された, 離ればなれの ②[話・考えなどが]まとまりのない

□ **discuss** 動議論[検討]する

□ **Disneyland** 名ディズニーランド

□ **dispose** 動①処理する, 捨てる ②配置する

□ **dive** 動①飛び込む, もぐる ②急降下する[させる] 名飛び込み, ダイビング

□ **divorce** 動離婚する 名離婚, 分離

□ **do** 熟 do a good job うまくやってのける do one's best 全力を尽くす do well うまくいく, 成功する do with one's life 人生を費やす

□ **dock** 名ドック, 造船所, 波止場, 埠頭 動①ドックに入れる, ドックに入る ②(宇宙船を)ドッキングする

□ **documentary** 名(映画・テレビなどの)ドキュメンタリー 形文書の, 記録による

□ **don't** 熟 don't have to do ～する必要はない

□ **doubt** 名①疑い, 不確かなこと ②未解決点, 困難 動疑う

□ **down** 熟 let oneself down 落ち込む, 失望させる lie down 横たわる, 横になる slow down 速度を落とす write down 書き留める

□ **drain** 名①排水管, 下水溝 ②消耗 動①(水が)流れる ②(水が)引く ③水抜きをする, 排出させる

□ **draw** 動①引く, 引っ張る ②描く ③引き分けになる[する]

□ **drawing** 動 draw (引く)の現在分詞 名①素描, 製図 ②引くこと

□ **driven** 動 drive (車で行く)の過去分詞

□ **driving** 動 drive (車で行く)の現在分詞 名運転 形①推進する, 精力的な ②運転用の

E

□ **each one of us** 人は誰しも

□ **each other** お互いに

□ **eagerly** 副熱心に, しきりに

□ **earn** 動①儲ける, 稼ぐ ②(名声を)博す

□ **ease** 名安心, 気楽 with ease 容易に, やすやすと 動安心させる, 楽にする, ゆるめる

□ **easily** 副①容易に, たやすく, 苦もなく ②気楽に

□ **edit** 動編集する

□ **education** 名教育, 教養

□ **effect** 名①影響, 効果, 結果 ②実施, 発効 動もたらす, 達成する

□ **effective** 形効果的である, 有効である

□ **else** 熟 no one else 他の誰一人として～しない

□ **email** 名電子メール

□ **emotion** 名感激, 感動, 感情

□ **empathy** 名共感, 感情移入

□ **enable** 動(～することを)可能にする, 容易にする

□ **encourage** 動①勇気づける ②促進する, 助長する

□ **end** 熟 at the end of ～の終わりに

□ **engage** 動①約束する, 婚約する ②雇う, 従事する[させる],《be -d in》～に従事している

□ **enjoy doing** ～するのが好きだ, ～するのを楽しむ

□ **enjoyable** 形楽しめる，愉快な

□ **enough to do** ～するのに十分な

□ **enrich** 動豊かにする，充実させる

□ **enrichment** 名豊かにすること，価値を高めること，栄養価を高めること，濃縮

□ **enthusiastic** 形熱狂的な，熱烈な

□ **envious** 形うらやんで

□ **equal** 形等しい，均等な，平等な 動匹敵する，等しい 名同等のもの［人］

□ **equally** 副等しく，平等に

□ **even if** たとえ～でも

□ **even though** ～であるけれども，～にもかかわらず

□ **eventually** 副結局は

□ **ever** 熟 more than ever ますます，これまで以上に

□ **every day** 毎日

□ **every time** ～するときはいつも

□ **everyday** 形毎日の，日々の

□ **everyone** 代誰でも，皆

□ **everything** 代すべてのこと［もの］，何でも，何もかも

□ **examine** 動試験する，調査［検査］する，診察する

□ **example** 熟 for example たとえば

□ **excited** 動 excite（興奮する）の過去，過去分詞 形興奮した，わくわくした

□ **excitement** 名興奮（すること）

□ **exciting** 動 excite（興奮する）の現在分詞 形興奮させる，わくわくさせる

□ **exercise** 名①運動，体操 ②練習 動①運動する，練習する ②影響を及ぼす

□ **exist** 動存在する，生存する，ある，いる

□ **expand** 動①広げる，拡張［拡大］する ②発展させる，拡充する

□ **expect** 動予期［予測］する，(当然のこととして) 期待する

□ **extend** 動①伸ばす，延長［延期］する ②(範囲が) およぶ，広がる，(期間などが) わたる

F

□ **Facebook** 名フェイスブック《SNS の商標》

□ **fail** 動①失敗する，落第する［させる］②《- to ～》～し損なう，～できない ③失望させる 名失敗，落第点

□ **failure** 名①失敗，落第 ②不足，欠乏 ③停止，減退

□ **fair** 形①正しい，公平［正当］な ②快晴の ③色白の，金髪の ④かなりの ⑤《古》美しい 副①公平に，きれいに ②見事に

□ **fat** 形①太った ②脂っこい ③分厚い 名脂肪，肥満

□ **fear** 名①恐れ ②心配，不安 動①恐れる ②心配する

□ **feed** 動①食物を与える ②供給する 名①飼育，食事 ②供給

□ **feel better** 気分がよくなる

□ **feel good** 気持ちいい，心地よい

□ **feel like** ～のような感じがする

□ **feeling** 動 feel（感じる）の現在分詞 名①感じ，気持ち ②触感，知覚 ③同情，思いやり，感受性 形感じる，感じやすい，情け深い

□ **fiction** 名フィクション，作り話，小説

□ **filled with** 《be - 》～でいっぱいになる

□ **filling** 動 fill（満ちる）の現在分詞 名①(歯の) 充填剤 ②(パンなどの) 詰め物，中身 形食べごたえのある

□ **filmmaker** 名映画製作者，映像作

家

□ **find out** 見つけ出す, 知る, 調べる

□ **finding** 動find (見つける)の現在分詞 名①発見 《-s》発見物, 調査結果 《-s》認定, 決定, 答申

□ **first** 熟at first 最初は, 初めのうちは for the first time 初めて

□ **fix** 動①固定する[させる] ②修理する ③決定する ④用意する, 整える

□ **flash** 名閃光, きらめき 動①閃光を発する ②さっと動く, ひらめく

□ **flight** 名飛ぶこと, 飛行, (飛行機の)フライト take flight 逃げる

□ **flow** 動流れ出る, 流れる, あふれる 名①流出 ②流ちょう(なこと)

□ **flying** 動fly (飛ぶ)の現在分詞 名飛行 形飛んでいる, 空中に浮かぶ, (飛ぶように)速い

□ **focus** 名①焦点, ピント ②関心の的, 着眼点 ③中心 動①焦点を合わせる ②(関心・注意を)集中させる focus on ～に重点を置く, ～に心を注ぐ

□ **following** 動follow (ついていく)の現在分詞 形《the –》次の, 次に続く 名《the –》下記のもの, 以下に述べるもの

□ **for** 熟ask for help 助けを頼む care for ～の世話をする, ～を大事に思う for a moment 少しの間 for a while しばらくの間, 少しの間 for example たとえば for oneself 独力で, 自分のために for the first time 初めて for ～ years ～年間, ～年にわたって go for ～を追い求める go for a walk 散歩に行く grateful for 《be –》～に感謝している It is ～ for someone to … (人)が…するのは～だ look for ～を探す reach for ～に手を伸ばす reason for ～の理由 thanks to someone for ～のことで(人)に感謝する wait for ～を待つ

□ **forgive** 動許す, 免除する

□ **forgiveness** 名許す(こと), 寛容

□ **forgiving** 動forgive (許す)の現在分詞 形〔人の罪・非礼などに〕寛大な, 寛容な

□ **form** 名①形, 形式 ②書式 動形づくる

□ **forward** 形①前方の, 前方へ向かう ②将来の ③先の 副①前方に ②将来に向けて ③先へ, 進んで look forward to ～を楽しみに待つ 動①転送する ②進める 名前衛

□ **founder** 名創立者, 設立者

□ **fragile** 形壊れやすい, もろい, 傷つきやすい

□ **freeze** 動①凍る, 凍らせる ②ぞっとする[させる]

□ **Friday** 名金曜日

□ **friendly** 形親しみのある, 親切な, 友情のこもった 副友好的に, 親切に

□ **friendship** 名友人であること, 友情

□ **frightened** 動frighten (驚かせる)の過去, 過去分詞 形おびえた, びっくりした

□ **from** 熟cut someone off from (人)を～から切り離す from ～ to … ～から…まで keep someone from ～から(人)を阻む move away from ～から遠ざかる stay away from ～から離れている

□ **fully** 副十分に, 完全に, まるまる

□ **fundamental** 名基本, 原理 形基本の, 根本的な, 重要な

□ **future** 熟in the future 将来は

G

□ **gain** 動①得る, 増す ②進歩する, 進む 名①増加, 進歩 ②利益, 得ること, 獲得

□ **generous** 形①寛大な, 気前のよい ②豊富な

□ **gentle** 形①優しい, 温和な ②柔らかな

□ **gentleness** 名 優しさ, 親切

□ **gently** 副 親切に, 上品に, そっと, 優しく

□ **get** 熟 get along with (人) と仲良くする, 歩調を合わせる get back 戻る, 帰る get better 良くなる, 上達する get in the way 邪魔をする, 妨げになる get in touch with ～に触れる, 感じる get it right きちんと決着をつける get out of bed 起きる, 寝床を離れる get ready to ～する用意[支度] をする get stuck in ～にはまり込む get through 乗り切る, ～を通り抜ける

□ **gift** 名 ①贈り物 ②(天賦の) 才能 動 授ける

□ **give out** 分配する

□ **give up** あきらめる, 引き渡す

□ **glide** 動 滑る, 滑るように動く 名 滑走, 滑空

□ **globally** 副 グローバルに, 地球規模で, 世界レベルで

□ **go** 熟 come and go 行き来する, 現れては消える go ahead with 〔計画・仕事などを〕進める go for ～を追い求める go for a walk 散歩に行く go into ～に入る, ～にぶつかる go on 続く, 進み続ける, 起こる go out of one's way to ～するために力を尽くす go through 通り抜ける, 経験する go to sleep 寝る go wrong 失敗する, 道を踏みはずす let go 自由になる, 解放する let go of ～を解き放つ, 取り除く

□ **good** 熟 do a good job うまくやってのける feel good 気持ちいい, 心地よい

□ **good-enough** 形 十分によい, 間に合う, 通用する

□ **goodbye** 熟 say goodbye to ～にさよならと言う

□ **goodness** 名 ①善良さ, よいところ ②優秀 ③神《婉曲表現》

□ **gracious** 形 ①親切な, ていねいな ②慈悲深い ③優雅な 間 おや! ま

あ!

□ **graciousness** 名 上品さ, ていねいさ, 寛大さ, 優雅さ

□ **grass** 名 草, 牧草 (地), 芝生 動 草 [芝生] で覆う [覆われる]

□ **grateful** 形 感謝する, ありがたく思う grateful for《be –》～に感謝している

□ **gratitude** 名 感謝 (の気持ち), 報恩の念

□ **greet** 動 ①あいさつする ②(喜んで) 迎える

□ **grow into** 成長して～になる

□ **guidance** 名 案内, 手引き, 指導

□ **guilt** 名 罪 有罪 犯罪

H

□ **handling** 動 handle (手を触れる) の現在分詞 名 ①取り扱い, 処理 ② (サッカーなどでの) ハンド

□ **happen to** たまたま～する, 偶然～する

□ **happening** 動 happen (起こる) の現在分詞 名 出来事, 事件

□ **happiness** 名 幸せ, 喜び

□ **happy to do** 《be –》～してうれしい, 喜んで～する

□ **hard time** 《a –》つらい時期

□ **hard to** ～し難い

□ **hate** 動 嫌う, 憎む, (～するのを) いやがる 名 憎しみ

□ **have** 熟 could have done ～だったかもしれない《仮定法》 don't have to do ～する必要はない have an influence over ～に影響を及ぼす have power over ～を支配する力を持っている should have done ～すべきだった (のにしなかった)《仮定法》

□ **head** 動 〔ある方向に〕進む, 行く

□ **heal** 動 いえる, いやす, 治る, 治す

□ **healing** 動 heal (いえる) の現在分詞 形 治療の, 病気を治す, いやす 名 治療

□ **health-giving** 形 健康を増進させる

□ **healthy** 形 健康な, 健全な, 健康によい

□ **hear about** ～について聞く

□ **hearing** 動 hear (聞く) の現在分詞 名 ①聞くこと, 聴取, 聴力 ②聴聞会, ヒアリング

□ **heartbeat** 名 心臓の鼓動, 心拍 **in a heartbeat** すぐに, 一瞬で

□ **heartbroken** 形 悲しみに打ちひしがれた

□ **help** 熟 **ask for help** 助けを頼む **help ～ to …** ～が…するのを助ける **help ～ with …** …を～の面で手伝う

□ **helpful** 形 役に立つ, 参考になる

□ **helpfulness** 名 助けになること, 有用性

□ **helping** 動 help (助ける) の現在分詞 名 ①助力, 手助け ②(食べ物の) ひと盛り, 1杯, お代わり 形 救いの, 助けの

□ **hem** 名 へり, 縁

□ **here are ～** こちらは～です。

□ **hidden** 動 hide (隠れる) の過去分詞 形 隠れた, 秘密の

□ **hide** 動 隠れる, 隠す, 隠れて見えない, 秘密にする

□ **hold on to** ～をつかんで放さない

□ **home** 熟 **at home** 自宅で, くつろいで

□ **honest** 形 ①正直な, 誠実な, 心からの ②公正な, 感心な

□ **honestly** 副 正直に

□ **honesty** 名 正直, 誠実

□ **honor** 名 ①名誉, 光栄, 信用 ②節操, 自尊心 動 尊敬する, 栄誉を与える

□ **hope-filled** 形 〔未来・人生などが〕希望に満ちた

□ **hopeful** 形 希望に満ちた, 望みを抱いて (いる), 有望な

□ **hopeless** 形 ①希望のない, 絶望的な ②勝ち目のない

□ **how** 熟 **how to** ～する方法 **no matter how** どんなに～であろうとも **show ～ how to …** ～に…のやり方を示す

□ **however** 副 たとえ～でも 接 けれども, だが

□ **hug** 名 抱き締めること 動 しっかりと抱き締める

□ **humanitarian** 形 人道主義の, 博愛の 名 人道主義者, 博愛主義者, ヒューマニスト

□ **humor** 名 ①ユーモア ②(一時的な) 機嫌 動 機嫌をとる

□ **hundreds of** 何百もの～

□ **hurry** 熟 **in a hurry** 急いで, あわてて

□ **hurtful** 形 傷つける, 有害な

I

□ **if** 熟 **If ＋《主語》＋ could** ～できればなあ《仮定法》 **as if** あたかも～のように, まるで～みたいに **ask ～ if** ～かどうか尋ねる **even if** たとえ～でも

□ **image** 名 ①印象, 姿 ②画像, 映像 動 心に描く, 想像する

□ **imagination** 名 想像 (力), 空想

□ **imagine** 動 想像する, 心に思い描く

□ **impact** 名 影響力, 反響, 効果 動 ①詰め込む ②衝突する

□ **impeccable** 形 欠点のない, 完璧な

□ **improve** 動 改善する [させる], 進歩する

□ **in** 熟 in a heartbeat すぐに, 一瞬で in a hurry 急いで, あわてて in a way ～な方法で, ある意味では in control ～を支配して, ～を掌握している in order to ～するために, ～しようと in some way 何とかして, 何らかの方法で in spite of ～にもかかわらず in the future 将来は in the world 世界で in this way このようにして

□ **include** 動 含む, 勘定に入れる

□ **increase** 動 増加[増強]する, 増やす, 増える 名 増加(量), 増大

□ **indelible** 形 消せない, 忘れられない

□ **influence** 名 影響, 勢力 have an influence over ～に影響を及ぼす 動 影響をおよぼす

□ **inner** 形 ①内部の ②心の中の

□ **insecure** 形 不安定な, 心細い

□ **inspiration** 名 霊感, ひらめき, 妙案, 吸気

□ **inspire** 動 ①奮い立たせる, 鼓舞する ②(感情などを)吹き込む ③霊感を与える

□ **inspired** 動 inspire(奮い立たせる)の過去, 過去分詞 形 霊感を受けた, 心を動かされた

□ **Instagram** 名 インスタグラム《SNSの商標》

□ **instead** 副 その代わりに instead of ～の代わりに, ～をしないで

□ **interest** 熟 show interest in ～に興味を示す, ～に関心を見せる

□ **into** 熟 come into one's mind (人)の心に浮かんでくる go into ～に入る, ～にぶつかる grow into 成長して～になる put ～ into … ～を…の状態にする, ～を…に突っ込む turn into ～に変わる

□ **introduction** 名 紹介, 導入

□ **intuition** 名 直感, 洞察

□ **issue** 名 ①問題, 論点 ②発行物 ③出口, 流出 動 ①(～から)出る, 生じ

る ②発行する

□ **it** 熟 It is up to you to do ～するのはあなた次第だ It is ～ for someone to … (人)が…するのは～だ it's over 終わる get it right きちんと決着をつける

□ **item** 名 ①項目, 品目 ②(新聞などの)記事

J

□ **Japan** 名 日本《国名》

□ **jealous** 形 嫉妬して, 嫉妬深い, うらやんで

□ **jealousy** 名 嫉妬, ねたみ

□ **job** 熟 do a good job うまくやってのける

□ **join in** 加わる, 参加する

□ **journal** 名 雑誌, 機関誌, 日誌

□ **journaling** 名 〔行動・アイデア・確認事項を〕記録[表現]すること

□ **journalist** 名 報道関係者, ジャーナリスト

□ **journey** 名 ①(遠い目的地への)旅 ②行程

□ **joy** 名 喜び, 楽しみ with joy 喜んで

□ **joyful** 形 楽しませる, 喜びに満ちた

□ **judgment** 名 ①判断, 意見 ②裁判, 判決

□ **just as** (ちょうど)であろうとおり

K

□ **keep someone from** ～から(人)を阻む

□ **keep up with** ～に遅れずについていく, 歩調を合わせる

□ **kind of** ある程度, ～のようなもの

□ **kind to** 《be –》～に親切である

A
B
C
D
E
F
G
H
I
J
K
L
M
N
O
P
Q
R
S
T
U
V
W
X
Y
Z

□ **kindly** 形 ①親切な, 情け深い, 思いやりのある ②(気候などの)温和な, 快い 副 親切に, 優しく

□ **kindness** 名 親切(な行為), 優しさ

□ **knowing** 動 know (知っている) の現在分詞 形 物知りの, 故意の

□ **knowledge** 名 知識, 理解, 学問

L

□ **latest** 形 ①最新の, 最近の ②最も遅い 副 最も遅く, 最後に

□ **leadership** 名 指揮, リーダーシップ

□ **leaning** 動 lean (もたれる) の現在分詞 名 ①傾き ②傾向, 好み

□ **least** 形 いちばん小さい, 最も少ない 副 いちばん小さく, 最も少なく 名 最小, 最少 **at least** 少なくとも

□ **leave behind** あとにする, ～を置き去りにする

□ **less** 形 ～より小さい[少ない] 副 ～より少なく, ～ほどでなく

□ **lessen** 動 (物, 事を) 少なく[小さく]する, 減らす

□ **let go** 自由になる, 解放する

□ **let go of** ～を解き放つ, 取り除く

□ **let oneself down** 落ち込む, 失望させる

□ **level** 名 ①水平, 平面 ②水準 形 ①水平の, 平たい ②同等[同位]の 動 ①水平にする ②平等にする

□ **lie** 動 ①うそをつく ②横になる, 寝る ③(ある状態に)ある, 存在する **lie down** 横たわる, 横になる 名 うそ, 詐欺

□ **life** 熟 **do with one's life** 人生を費やす

□ **light-brown** 形 薄茶の, 明るい茶色の

□ **lighten** 動 ①明るくする, 明るく

なる ②軽くする, 楽になる

□ **like** 熟 **Would you like to ～?** ～をしたいですか。 **feel like** ～のような感じがする **like this** このような, こんなふうに **would like** ～がほしい **would like to** ～したいと思う

□ **likely** 形 ①ありそうな, (～)しそうな ②適当な 副 たぶん, おそらく

□ **liking** 動 like (好む) の現在分詞 名 好み, 趣味

□ **limit** 名 限界, 《-s》範囲, 境界 動 制限[限定]する

□ **liner** 名 ①定期船, 定期旅客機 ②(野球の)ライナー

□ **link** 名 ①(鎖の)輪 ②リンク ③相互[因果]関係 動 連結する, つながる

□ **list** 名 名簿, 目録, 一覧表 動 名簿[目録]に記入する

□ **listener** 名 聞く人, ラジオ聴取者

□ **literary** 形 文学の, 文芸の

□ **live up to** (期待などに) 沿う, (基準などに)したがって行動する

□ **living** 動 live (住む) の現在分詞 名 生計, 生活 形 ①生きている, 現存の ②使用されている ③そっくりの

□ **locally** 副 ①ある特定の場所[地方]で, 現地的に ②近くで, このあたりで

□ **logic** 名 論理(学), 理屈

□ **logical** 形 論理学の, 論理的な

□ **lonely** 形 ①孤独な, 心さびしい ②ひっそりした, 人里離れた

□ **long-held** 形 長年抱いてきた, かねての

□ **look** 熟 **look after** ～の世話をする, ～に気をつける **look for** ～を探す **look forward to** ～を楽しみに待つ **look to** ～を目指す, ～の方を向く

□ **lose sight of** ～を見失う

□ **lot** 名 《a - of / - s of》たくさんの～

□ **loving** 動 love (愛する) の現在分詞 形 愛する, 愛情のこもった

☐ **luxury** 形豪華な, 高級な, 贅沢な 名豪華さ, 贅沢（品）

M

☐ **magic** 名①魔法, 手品 ②魔力 形魔法の, 魔力のある

☐ **magnificent** 形壮大な, 壮麗な, すばらしい

☐ **make a mistake** 間違いをする

☐ **make sense of** ～の意味を理解する

☐ **make sure** 確かめる, 確実に～する

☐ **making** 動 make（作る）の現在分詞 名制作, 製造

☐ **manage** 動①動かす, うまく処理する ②経営［管理］する, 支配する ③どうにか～する

☐ **mark** 名①印, 記号, 跡 ②点数 ③特色 動①印［記号］をつける ②採点する ③目立たせる

☐ **mask** 名面, マスク 動マスクをつける

☐ **massage** 名マッサージ 動マッサージする

☐ **match** 名①試合, 勝負 ②相手, 釣り合うもの ③マッチ（棒）動①～に匹敵する ②調和する, 釣り合う ③（～を…と）勝負させる

☐ **matter** 熟 no matter how どんなに～であろうとも no matter what たとえ何があろう［起ころう］と

☐ **measure** 動①測る,（～の）寸法がある ②評価する 名①寸法, 測定, 計量, 単位 ②程度, 基準

☐ **media** 名メディア, マスコミ, 媒体

☐ **meditate** 動深く考える, 瞑想する

☐ **meditation** 名瞑想, 黙想

☐ **meeting** 動 meet（会う）の現在分詞 名①集まり, ミーティング, 面会

②競技会

☐ **memory** 名①記憶（力）, 思い出 ②（コンピューターの）メモリ, 記憶装置

☐ **Michelle Pfeiffer** ミシェル・ファイファー《アメリカの女優, 1958 - 》

☐ **might** 助《may の過去》①～かもしれない ②～してもよい, ～できる 名力, 権力

☐ **mind** 名①心, 精神, 考え ②知性 come into one's mind（人）の心に浮かんでくる 動①気にする, いやがる ②気をつける, 用心する

☐ **mindfulness** 名マインドフルネス

☐ **missing** 動 miss（失敗する）の現在分詞 形欠けている, 行方不明の 名《the – 》行方不明者

☐ **mistake** 熟 make a mistake 間違いをする

☐ **moment** 名①瞬間, ちょっとの間 ②（特定の）時, 時期 at any moment 今すぐにも at the moment 今は for a moment 少しの間

☐ **more** 熟 more of ～よりもっと more than ～を超える, ～以上 more than ever ますます, これまで以上に the more ～ the more … ～すればするほどますます…

☐ **most of the time** たいていの場合, ほとんどの時間

☐ **mostly** 副主として, 多くは, ほとんど

☐ **motivate** 動動機付ける, 刺激する

☐ **move away from** ～から遠ざかる

☐ **move on** 先に進む

☐ **movement** 名①動き, 運動 ②《-s》行動 ③引っ越し ④変動

☐ **moving** 動 move（動く）の現在分詞 形①動いている ②感動させる

☐ **much** 熟 too much 過度に

143

A
B
C
D
E
F
G
H
I
J
K
L
M
N
O
P
Q
R
S
T
U
V
W
X
Y
Z

□ **muscle** 图筋肉, 腕力 動強引に押し進む, 力ずくで進む

N

□ **nature** 熟 by nature 生まれつき

□ **nearly** 副 ①近くに, 親しく ②ほとんど, あやうく

□ **need to do** ～する必要がある

□ **needy** 形貧乏な, お金に困って, すがるような

□ **negative** 形 ①否定的な, 消極的な ②負の, マイナスの, (写真が)ネガの 图 ①否定, 反対 ②ネガ, 陰画, 負数, マイナス

□ **negativity** 图後ろ向きなこと, 消極性

□ **negotiate** 動交渉[協議]する

□ **network** 图回路, 網状組織, ネットワーク

□ **news** 图報道, ニュース, 便り, 知らせ

□ **newspaper** 图新聞(紙)

□ **next time** 次回に, この次～するときは

□ **no** 熟 no matter how どんなに～であろうとも no matter what たとえ何があろう[起ころう]と no one 誰も～ない no one else 他の誰一人として～しない

□ **none** 代(～の)何も[誰も・少しも]…ない

□ **normal** 形普通の, 平均の, 標準的な 图平常, 標準, 典型

□ **not** 熟 not always 必ずしも～であるとは限らない not at all 少しも～でない not quite まったく～だというわけではない not ～ but … ～ではなくて

□ **note** 图 ①メモ, 覚え書き ②注釈 ③注意, 注目 ④手形 動 ①書き留める ②注意[注目]する

□ **notebook** 图ノート, 手帳

□ **notice** 图 ①注意 ②通知 ③公告 動 ①気づく, 認める ②通告する

□ **noticeboard** 图掲示板, 告知板

□ **now** 熟 right now 今すぐに, たった今

□ **nurse** 图 ①看護師[人] ②乳母 動 ①看病する ②あやす

□ **nurture** 動養育する, 育てる 图養育

□ **nurturing** 图育てること, 養育, 育成

O

□ **occur** 動(事が)起こる, 生じる, (考えなどが)浮かぶ

□ **of value** 貴重な, 価値のある

□ **off** 熟 cut off 切断する, 切り離す cut someone off from (人)を～から切り離す put off 意欲を失わせる, 不快にさせる set off 引き起こす, 急に～させる turn off ～を止める, (照明などを)消す

□ **offer** 動申し出る, 申し込む, 提供する 图提案, 提供

□ **OK** 形《許可・同意・満足などを表して。O.K.とも》よろしい, 正しい 图許可, 承認 動オーケー[承認]する

□ **Oliver** 图オリバー《人名》

□ **on** 熟 build on ～の上に築く, ～を基にして前進する depend on ～次第である focus on ～に重点を置く, ～に心を注ぐ go on 続く, 進み続ける, 起こる hold on to ～をつかんで放さない move on 先に進む on (the) average 平均して on purpose わざと, 意図的に rest on ～の上に横たわる sit on ～の上に座る

□ **one** 熟 each one of us 人は誰しも no one 誰も～ない no one else 他の誰一人として～しない one of ～

の1つ[人]

- **oneself** 熟 **for oneself** 独力で, 自分のために **let oneself down** 落ち込む, 失望させる **true to oneself**《be –》自分自身に対して忠実[誠実]である

- **online** 名 オンライン 形 オンラインの, ネットワーク上の

- **open air** 戸外, 野外

- **open up the possibility of** ~の可能性を広げる

- **opening** 動 open（開く）の現在分詞 名 ①開始, 始め ②開いた所, 穴 ③空き, 欠員 形 開始の, 最初の, 開会の

- **openness** 名 開放, 公開

- **operate** 動 ①（機械などが）動く, 運転する, 管理する, 操業する ②作用する ③手術する

- **opposite** 形 反対の, 向こう側の 前 ~の向こう側に 名 反対の人[物]

- **optimism** 名 楽天主義, 楽観

- **optimistic** 形 楽観的な

- **order** 熟 **in order to** ~するために, ~しようと

- **other** 熟 **each other** お互いに

- **otherwise** 副 さもないと, そうでなければ

- **out** 熟 **cut out** 切り取る, 切り抜く **find out** 見つけ出す, 知る, 調べる **get out of bed** 起きる, 寝床を離れる **give out** 分配する **go out of one's way to** ~するために力を尽くす **out of** ~から外へ, ~から抜け出して **take time out** 小休止する, 時間をとる[つくる] **try to talk someone out of** (人)に~をやめるよう説得する **work out** うまくいく, 考え出す, ~の結果になる

- **outlook** 名 ①見通し, 見解 ②見晴らし

- **over** 熟 **all over the world** 世界中に **have an influence over** ~に影響を及ぼす **have power over** ~を

支配する力を持っている **it's over** 終わる **over time** 時間とともに, そのうち

- **over-talking** 名 話し過ぎること, 過剰なおしゃべり

- **overcome** 動 勝つ, 打ち勝つ, 克服する

- **owner** 名 持ち主, オーナー

P

- **pace** 名 歩調, 速度 動 ゆっくり歩く, 行ったり来たりする

- **paddle** 名 水かき, 櫂, へら 動 櫂で漕ぐ

- **paid** 動 pay（払う）の過去, 過去分詞 形 有給の, 支払い済みのの

- **painful** 形 ①痛い, 苦しい, 痛ましい ②骨の折れる, 困難な

- **pandemic** 名 パンデミック《世界的な感染病の大流行》

- **parent** 名《-s》両親

- **partner** 名 配偶者, 仲間, 同僚 動 (~と)組む, 提携する

- **passion** 名 情熱,（~への）熱中, 激怒

- **passionate** 形 情熱的な,（感情が）激しい, 短気な

- **past** 形 過去の, この前の 名 過去（の出来事）前《時間・場所》~を過ぎて, ~を越して 副 通り越して, 過ぎて

- **path** 名 ①（踏まれてできた）小道, 歩道 ②進路, 通路

- **patience** 名 我慢, 忍耐（力）, 根気

- **patiently** 副 我慢強く, 根気よく

- **pay** 動 ①支払う, 払う, 報いる, 償う ②割に合う, ペイする **pay attention to** ~に注意を払う 名 給料, 報い

- **peaceful** 形 平和な, 穏やかな

- **pebble** 名 ①小石 ②水晶

□ **penny** 名①ペニー、ペンス《英国の貨幣単位。1/100ポンド》②《否定文で》小銭、びた一文

□ **perseverance** 名忍耐(力)、根気

□ **personal** 形①個人の、私的な ②本人自らの

□ **personally** 副個人的には、自分で

□ **philosopher** 名哲学者、賢者

□ **photo** 名写真

□ **phrase** 名句、慣用句、名言 動言葉で言い表す

□ **physical** 形①物質の、物理学の、自然科学の ②身体の、肉体の

□ **pick up** 拾い上げる

□ **pizza** 名ピザ

□ **planning** 動plan(計画する)の現在分詞 名立案、開発計画

□ **play with** ～で遊ぶ、～と一緒に遊ぶ

□ **playfulness** 名遊び好きなこと、陽気であること

□ **pleased** 動please(喜ばす)の過去、過去分詞 形喜んだ、気に入った

□ **pleasure** 名喜び、楽しみ、満足、娯楽

□ **political** 形①政治の、政党の ②策略的な

□ **positive** 形①前向きな、肯定的な、好意的な ②明確な、明白な、確信している ③プラスの 名①正数、プラス、陽極 ②ポジ、陽画

□ **positively** 副明確に、確かに、積極的に

□ **positivity** 名明瞭さ、積極性

□ **possibility** 名可能性、見込み、将来性 open up the possibility of ～の可能性を広げる

□ **possible** 形①可能な ②ありうる、起こりうる as ～ as possible できるだけ～ what is possible 何が[どこまで]できるのか

□ **postscript** 名①(手紙の)追伸 ②(書物・論文などの)後記、あとがき

□ **power** 熟 have power over ～を支配する力を持っている

□ **powerful** 形力強い、実力のある、影響力のある

□ **pregnant** 形妊娠している

□ **prepared** 形準備[用意]のできた

□ **pretend** 動①ふりをする、装う ②あえて～しようとする

□ **preview** 動下見する、前もって見る

□ **probably** 副たぶん、あるいは

□ **problem-solving** 名問題解決 形問題解決の

□ **professionalism** 名プロ根性、専門家気質[技術]

□ **progress** 名①進歩、前進 ②成り行き、経過 動前進する、上達する

□ **proverb** 名ことわざ、格言

□ **psychologist** 名心理学者、精神分析医

□ **purpose** 熟 on purpose わざと、意図的に

□ **pursue** 動①追う、つきまとう ②追求する、従事する

□ **put ～ into ...** ～を…の状態にする、～を…に突っ込む

□ **put off** 意欲を失わせる、不快にさせる

□ **puzzle** 名①難問、当惑 ②パズル 動迷わせる、当惑する[させる]

Q

□ **quality** 名①質、性質、品質 ②特性 ③良質

□ **quarrel** 名けんか、争論、不和 動けんかする、口論する

□ **quickly** 副敏速に、急いで

□ **quietly** 副①静かに ②平穏に、控えめに

□ **quite** 熟 not quite まったく~だというわけではない

□ **quote** 動 ①引用する ②（価格などを）見積もる 名 ①引用（句）②見積もり

R

□ **raise** 動 ①上げる，高める ②起こす ③~を育てる ④（資金を）調達する 名 高める［上げる］こと，昇給

□ **rarely** 副 めったに~しない，まれに，珍しいほど

□ **rather** 副 ①むしろ，かえって ②かなり，いくぶん，やや ③それどころか逆に rather than ~よりむしろ

□ **re-live** 動 追体験する，思い出す

□ **reach for** ~に手を伸ばす

□ **react** 動 反応する，対処する

□ **reaction** 名 反応，反動，反抗，影響

□ **reader** 名 ①読者 ②読本，リーダー

□ **reading** 動 read（読む）の現在分詞 名 読書，読み物，朗読

□ **ready** 熟 get ready to ~する用意［支度］をする

□ **real-life** 形 ①現実の［に起きている］，実際の ②（人物などが）実在の

□ **reality** 名 現実，実在，真実（性）

□ **reason for** ~の理由

□ **receiving** 名 受け取ること

□ **reconnect** 動 再びつながる，再接続される

□ **record** 名 ①記録，登録，履歴 ②（音楽などの）レコード 動 ①記録［登録］する ②録音［録画］する

□ **reduce** 動 ①減じる ②しいて~させる，（~の）状態にする

□ **reflect** 動 映る，反響する，反射する

□ **relationship** 名 関係，関連，血縁

関係

□ **relax** 動 ①くつろがせる ②ゆるめる，緩和する

□ **relaxation** 名 息抜き，くつろぎ，緩和，弛緩

□ **relaxed** 動 relax（くつろがせる）の過去，過去分詞 形 ①くつろいだ，ゆったりした ②ざっくばらんな

□ **rely** 動 （人が…に）頼る，当てにする

□ **remain** 動 ①残っている，残る ②（~の）ままである［いる］名 《-s》①残り（もの）②遺跡

□ **remedy** 名 治療（薬），改善（案）動 治療する，（状況を）改善する

□ **remind** 動 思い出させる，気づかせる

□ **repeat** 動 繰り返す 名 繰り返し，反復，再演

□ **reply** 動 答える，返事をする，応答する 名 答え，返事，応答

□ **require** 動 ①必要とする，要する ②命じる，請求する

□ **resentful** 形 憤慨した，怒った

□ **resilience** 名 ①弾性，復元力 ②回復力，立ち直る力

□ **resilient** 形 ①回復力のある，立ち直りが早い ②快活な

□ **resistance** 名 抵抗，反抗，敵対

□ **respect** 名 ①尊敬，尊重 ②注意，考慮 動 尊敬［尊重］する

□ **respectful** 形 礼儀正しい，ていねいな

□ **respond** 動 答える，返答［応答］する

□ **responsibility** 名 ①責任，義務，義理 ②負担，責務

□ **rest on** ~の上に横たわる

□ **result** 名 結果，成り行き，成績 as a result of ~の結果（として）動 （結果として）起こる，生じる，結局~になる

147

□ **reveal** 動明らかにする, 暴露する, もらす

□ **right** 熟get it right きちんと決着をつける　right now 今すぐに, たった今

□ **risk** 名危険 動危険にさらす, 賭ける, 危険をおかす

□ **risk-taking** 形リスクを負うような, 冒険する

□ **rubbish** 名ごみ, がらくた, くだらないこと

□ **run away** 走り去る, 逃げ出す

□ **rush** 動突進する, せき立てる　rush around trying to 〜で走り回る, 〜に急ぐ　名突進, 突撃, 殺到

S

□ **sacred** 形神聖な, 厳粛な

□ **sadness** 名悲しみ, 悲哀

□ **safely** 副安全に, 間違いなく

□ **safety** 名安全, 無事, 確実

□ **same** 熟the same 〜 as [that] …と同じ(ような)

□ **saving** 動save (救う)の現在分詞　名①節約 ②《-s》貯金 ③救助

□ **say goodbye to** 〜にさよならと言う

□ **saying** 動say (言う)の現在分詞　名ことわざ, 格言, 発言

□ **scan** 動ざっと目を通す, 細かく調べる, スキャンする　名スキャン, 精査

□ **scare** 動こわがらせる, おびえる　名恐れ, 不安

□ **scared** 動scare (こわがらせる)の過去, 過去分詞　形おびえた, びっくりした

□ **schooling** 名学校教育, 教室授業, スクーリング

□ **screen** 名仕切り, 幕, スクリーン, 画面　動①仕切る ②審査する ③上映する, 映画化する

□ **search** 動捜し求める, 調べる　名捜査, 探索, 調査

□ **searching** 動search (捜し求める)の現在分詞　形探るような, 徹底的な, 鋭い

□ **secondly** 副第2に, 次に

□ **security** 名①安全(性), 安心 ②担保, 抵当,《-ties》有価証券

□ **see 〜 as …** 〜を…と考える

□ **seek** 動捜し求める, 求める

□ **seem** 動(〜に)見える, (〜のように)思われる

□ **self** 名①自己, 〜そのもの ②私利, 私欲, 利己主義 ③自我

□ **self-awareness** 名自己認識, 自我の目覚め

□ **self-belief** 名自信, 自分を信じる心

□ **self-care** 名セルフケア, 自立, 自己療法

□ **self-confidence** 名自信

□ **self-discovery** 名自己発見

□ **self-esteem** 名自尊感情, 自己肯定感

□ **self-love** 名自己愛

□ **self-loving** 形身勝手な, きざな

□ **self-talk** 名独り言, 心の声

□ **sense** 名①感覚, 感じ ②《-s》意識, 正気, 本性 ③常識, 分別, センス ④意味　make sense of 〜の意味を理解する　動感じる, 気づく

□ **sentence** 名①文 ②判決, 宣告　動判決を下す, 宣告する

□ **separate** 動①分ける, 分かれる, 隔てる ②別れる, 別れさせる　形分かれた, 別れた, 別々の

□ **serve** 動①仕える, 奉仕する ②(客の)応対をする, 給仕する, 食事[飲み物]を出す ③(役目を)果たす, 務める, 役に立つ ④(球技で)サーブをする　名(球技で)サーブ(権)

- □ **service** 名①勤務, 業務 ②公益事業 ③点検, 修理 ④奉仕, 貢献 動保守点検する, (点検)修理をする

- □ **set off** 引き起こす, 急に～させる

- □ **sew** 動縫い物をする, 縫い付ける

- □ **shame** 名①恥, 恥辱 ②恥ずべきこと, ひどいこと 動恥をかかせる, 侮辱する

- □ **shape** 名①形, 姿, 型 ②状態, 調子 動形づくる, 具体化する

- □ **shift** 動移す, 変える, 転換する 名①変化, 移動 ②交替, (交代制の)勤務(時間), シフト

- □ **shine** 動①光る, 輝く ②光らせる, 磨く 名光, 輝き

- □ **shopping** 動shop(買い物をする)の現在分詞 名買い物

- □ **should have done** ～すべきだった(のにしなかった)《仮定法》

- □ **shoulder** 名肩 動肩にかつぐ, 肩で押し分けて進む

- □ **show ～ how to ...** ～に…のやり方を示す

- □ **show interest in** ～に興味を示す, ～に関心を見せる

- □ **shown** 動show(見せる)の過去分詞

- □ **shy** 形内気な, 恥ずかしがりの, 臆病な

- □ **side** 名側, 横, そば, 斜面 形①側面の, 横の ②副次的な 動(～の)側につく, 賛成する

- □ **sight** 熟lose sight of ～を見失う

- □ **signpost** 名道標, 手がかり

- □ **singing** 動sing(歌う)の現在分詞 名歌うこと, 歌声 形歌う, さえずる

- □ **sit on** ～の上に座る

- □ **sit up** 起き上がる, きちんと座る

- □ **situation** 名①場所, 位置 ②状況, 境遇, 立場

- □ **skill** 名①技能, 技術 ②上手, 熟練

- □ **sleep** 熟go to sleep 寝る

- □ **sleepy** 形①眠い, 眠そうな ②活気のない

- □ **slippery** 形つるつる滑る, 滑りやすい

- □ **slow down** 速度を落とす

- □ **smart** 形①利口な, 抜け目のない ②きちんとした, 洗練された ③激しい, ずきずきする 動ひりひり[ずきずき]痛む

- □ **smiling** 形微笑する, にこにこした

- □ **smother** 動①覆う, 包む ②窒息(死)させる, 息が詰まる

- □ **so ～ that ...** 非常に～なので

- □ **so that** ～するために, ～できるように

- □ **social** 形①社会の, 社会的な ②社交的な, 愛想のよい

- □ **solution** 名①分解, 溶解 ②解決, 解明, 回答

- □ **solve** 動解く, 解決する

- □ **some** 熟in some way 何とかして, 何らかの方法で

- □ **someone** 代ある人, 誰か

- □ **something** 代①ある物, 何か ②いくぶん, 多少

- □ **sometimes** 副時々, 時たま

- □ **somewhere** 副①どこかへ[に] ②いつか, およそ

- □ **soon** 熟as soon as ～するとすぐ, ～するや否や

- □ **soul** 名①魂 ②精神, 心

- □ **source** 名源, 原因, もと

- □ **Southampton** 名サウサンプトン《イギリスの地名》

- □ **speak of** ～を口にする

- □ **speak to** ～と話す

- □ **speaker** 名①話す人, 演説者, 代弁者 ②スピーカー, 拡声器 ③議長

- □ **speaking** 動speak(話す)の現在分詞 形話す, ものを言う 名話すこと, 談話, 演説

149

□ **spirit** 名①霊 ②精神, 気力

□ **spiritual** 形精神の, 精神的な, 霊的な

□ **spite** 名悪意, うらみ **in spite of** ～にもかかわらず

□ **spy** 名スパイ 動ひそかに見張る, スパイする

□ **stand up** 立ち上がる, 逆立つ

□ **start doing** ～し始める

□ **start to do** ～し始める

□ **state** 名①あり様, 状態 ②国家, (アメリカなどの)州 ③階層, 地位 動述べる, 表明する

□ **stay away from** ～から離れている

□ **stay in** (場所)にとどまる, (状態)を維持する

□ **stay with** ～に耐える[持ちこたえる]

□ **stop doing** ～するのをやめる

□ **stowaway** 名密航者

□ **streamer** 名吹き流し

□ **strength** 名①力, 体力 ②長所, 強み ③強度, 濃度

□ **stress** 名①圧力 ②ストレス ③強勢 動①強調する ②圧力を加える

□ **stressed** 形ストレスのかかった, ストレスに苦しんでいる

□ **stretch** 動引き伸ばす, 広がる, 広げる 名①伸ばす[伸びる]こと, 広がり ②ストレッチ(運動)

□ **struggle** 動もがく, 奮闘する 名もがき, 奮闘

□ **stuck** 動stick (刺さる)の過去, 過去分詞 **get stuck in** ～にはまり込む

□ **stupid** 形ばかな, おもしろくない

□ **success** 名成功, 幸運, 上首尾

□ **successful** 形成功した, うまくいった

□ **such as** たとえば～, ～のような

□ **sunshine** 名日光

□ **supermarket** 名スーパーマーケット

□ **support** 動①支える, 支持する ②養う, 援助する 名①支え, 支持 ②援助, 扶養

□ **supportive** 形支持するような

□ **supposed** 形～することになっている, ～しなければならない **supposed to**《be－》～することになっている, ～するはずである

□ **sure** 熟 **make sure** 確かめる, 確実に～する

□ **surf** 動①波に乗る ②(インターネットにアクセスして)ネットサーフィンをする 名打ち寄せる波

□ **surfing** 動surf (波に乗る)の現在分詞 名サーフィン

□ **survival** 名生き残ること, 生存者, 残存物

□ **survive** 動①生き残る, 存続する, なんとかなる ②長生きする, 切り抜ける

□ **sustainable** 形支えられる, 持続できる

□ **sustenance** 名(生命の)維持, 食物, 生計

□ **swan** 名ハクチョウ(白鳥)

□ **Sydney Harbour** 名シドニー・ハーバー《オーストラリアの地名》

T

□ **take** 熟 **take a break** 休息する **take a chance** 一か八かやってみる **take a deep breath in** 息を深く吸う **take a walk** 散歩する **take advantage of** ～を利用する, ～につけ込む **take flight** 逃げる **take time out** 小休止する, 時間をとる[つくる] **take ～ to do**〔…するために〕～を取る, ～を必要とする

□ **talent** 名才能, 才能ある人

□ **talk** 熟 **try to talk someone out**

of（人）に～をやめるよう説得する

□ **task** 名（やるべき）仕事, 職務, 課題 動仕事を課す, 負担をかける

□ **taste** 名①味, 風味 ②好み, 趣味 動味がする, 味わう

□ **teaching** 動 teach（教える）の現在分詞 名①教えること, 教授, 授業 ②《-s》教え, 教訓

□ **technology** 名テクノロジー, 科学技術

□ **teenager** 名 10代の人, ティーンエイジャー《13歳から19歳》

□ **television** 名テレビ

□ **tell ~ to ...** ～に…するように言う

□ **telling** 動 tell（話す）の現在分詞 形効果的な, 著しい

□ **tension** 名緊張（関係）, ぴんと張ること

□ **than** 熟 more than ～を超える, ～以上 more than ever ますます, これまで以上に rather than ～よりむしろ

□ **thankful** 形ありがたく思う

□ **thankless** 形①感謝されない, 報われない ②恩知らずの

□ **thanks to someone for** ～のことで（人）に感謝する

□ **that** 熟 so that ～するために, ～できるように so ~ that ... 非常に～なので…

□ **the more ~ the more ...** ～すればするほどますます…

□ **the same ~ as [that]...** …と同じ（ような）～

□ **think of** ～のことを考える

□ **thinking** 動 think（思う）の現在分詞 名考えること, 思考 形思考力のある, 考える

□ **this** 熟 in this way このようにして like this このような, こんなふうに this way このように

□ **though** 接①～にもかかわらず

ず, ～だが ②たとえ～でも **even though** ～であるけれども, ～にもかかわらず 副しかし

□ **thoughtful** 形思慮深い, 考え込んだ

□ **thoughtfully** 副考え[思いやり]深く

□ **thousands of** 何千という

□ **threat** 名おどし, 脅迫

□ **through** 熟 come through 通り抜ける get through 乗り切る, ～を通り抜ける go through 通り抜ける, 経験する

□ **Tibet** 名チベット《地名》

□ **tightly** 副きつく, しっかり, 堅く

□ **time** 熟 all the time いつも, その間ずっと at a time 一度に, 続けざまに at the time そのころ, 当時は by the time ～する時までに every time ～するときはいつも for the first time 初めて hard time《a－》つらい時期 most of the time たいていの場合, ほとんどの時間 next time 次回は, この次 ～するときは over time 時間とともに, そのうち take time out 小休止する, 時間をとる[つくる]

□ **timing** 名適時選択, タイミング

□ **tiny** 形ちっぽけな, とても小さい

□ **tip** 名①チップ, 心づけ ②先端, 頂点 動①チップをやる ②先端につける

□ **tired** 動 tire（疲れる）の過去, 過去分詞 形①疲れた, くたびれた ②飽きた, うんざりした **tired of**《be－》～に飽きて[うんざりして]いる

□ **tolerance** 名我慢, 寛容

□ **tone** 名音, 音色, 調子 動調和する[させる]

□ **too ~ to ...** …するには～すぎる

□ **too much** 過度に

□ **tool** 名道具, 用具, 工具

□ **touch** 熟 get in touch with ～に触れる, 感じる

151

□ **trained** 形訓練を受けた, 熟練した, 研鑽を積んだ

□ **trainer** 名トレーナー, 指導者

□ **transitory** 形一時的な, はかない, つかの間の

□ **treat** 動①扱う ②治療する ③おごる 名①おごり, もてなし, ごちそう ②楽しみ

□ **tribe** 名部族, 一族

□ **trigger** 名引き金, きっかけ, 要因 動引き起こす, もたらす

□ **true** 熟come true 実現する true to oneself《be－》自分自身に対して忠実[誠実]である

□ **truly** 副①全く, 本当に, 真に ②心から, 誠実に

□ **trust** 動信用[信頼]する, 委託する 名信用, 信頼, 委託

□ **trusted** 形信頼[信任]されている, 信用がある

□ **truth** 名①真理, 事実, 本当 ②誠実, 忠実さ

□ **try to talk someone out of** (人)に～をやめるよう説得する

□ **trying** 動try (やってみる)の現在分詞 rush around trying to ～で走り回る, ～に急ぐ 形つらい, 苦しい, しゃくにさわる

□ **tune** 名①曲, 節 ②正しい調子[旋律] 動①(ラジオ・テレビなどを)合わせる ②(楽器の)調子を合わせる

□ **turmoil** 名動揺, 騒動, 混乱

□ **turn** 熟turn around 向きを変える, 方向転換する turn into ～に変わる turn off ～を止める, (照明などを)消す turn to ～に変わる

□ **Twitter** 名ツイッター《SNSの商標》

U

□ **ugly** 形①醜い, ぶかっこうな ②いやな, 不快な, 険悪な

□ **unable** 形《be－to～》～することができない

□ **uncaring** 形気にかけない, 思いやりのない

□ **uncomfortable** 形心地よくない

□ **uncross** 動〔～の〕交差を解く

□ **underneath** 前～の下に, ～真下に 副下に[を], 根底は 名《the－》底部

□ **understanding** 動understand (理解する)の現在分詞 名理解, 意見の一致, 了解 形理解のある, 思いやりのある

□ **unfriendly** 形友情のない, 不親切な

□ **unhappy** 形不運な, 不幸な

□ **unique** 形唯一の, ユニークな, 独自の

□ **unkind** 形不親切な, 意地の悪い

□ **unkindness** 名不親切

□ **unless** 接もし～でなければ, ～しなければ

□ **unsafe** 形危険な, 安全でない

□ **untidy** 形きちんとしていない, だらしない

□ **up** 熟It is up to you to do ～するのはあなた次第だ caught up with ～にとらわれる, ～のとりこになる give up あきらめる, 引き渡す keep up with ～に遅れずについていく, 歩調を合わせる live up to (期待などに)沿う, (基準などに)したがって行動する open up the possibility of ～の可能性を広げる pick up 拾い上げる sit up 起き上がる, きちんと座る stand up 立ち上がる, 逆立つ wake up 起きる, 目を覚ます

□ **upon** 前①《場所・接触》～(の上)に ②《日・時》～に ③《関係・従事》～に関して, ～について, ～して 副前へ, 続けて

□ **upper** 形上の, 上位の, 北方の

- [ ] **urge** 動①せき立てる, 強力に推し進める, かりたてる ②《- to ～》…に～するよう熱心に勧める 名衝動, かりたてられるような気持ち
- [ ] **us** 熟each one of us 人は誰しも
- [ ] **used** 動①use (使う)の過去, 過去分詞 ②《- to ～》よく～したものだ, 以前は～であった 形①慣れている, 《get [become] - to》～に慣れてくる ②使われた, 中古の **used to**《be -》～に慣れる

V

- [ ] **valuable** 形貴重な, 価値のある, 役に立つ
- [ ] **value** 名価値, 値打ち, 価格 **of value** 貴重な, 価値のある 動評価する, 値をつける, 大切にする
- [ ] **value-driven** 形価値観によって動かされる
- [ ] **valued** 形高く評価された, 貴重な
- [ ] **version** 名①バージョン, 版, 翻訳 ②意見, 説明, 解釈
- [ ] **vision** 名①視力 ②先見, 洞察力
- [ ] **visualization** 名視覚化, 可視化
- [ ] **visualize** 動思い浮かべる, 心に描く, 想像する, 視覚化する

W

- [ ] **wait for** ～を待つ
- [ ] **waiting** 動wait (待つ)の現在分詞 名待機, 給仕すること 形待っている, 仕えている
- [ ] **wake up** 起きる, 目を覚ます
- [ ] **waking** 形〔眠らずに〕起きている, 覚醒している
- [ ] **walk** 熟go for a walk 散歩に行く **take a walk** 散歩をする
- [ ] **walking** 動walk (歩く)の現在分詞 名歩行, 歩くこと 形徒歩の, 歩行用の
- [ ] **wand** 名杖, 指揮棒
- [ ] **wanting** 動want (ほしい)の現在分詞 形欠けている
- [ ] **warmth** 名暖かさ, 思いやり
- [ ] **washing** 名洗濯
- [ ] **wave** 名①波 ②(手などを)振ること 動①揺れる, 揺らす, 波立つ ②(手などを振って)合図する
- [ ] **way** 熟by way of ～を手段として, ～のために **get in the way** 邪魔をする, 妨げになる **go out of one's way to** ～するために力を尽くす **in a way** ～な方法で, ある意味では **in some way** 何とかして, 何らかの方法で **in this way** このようにして **this way** このように **way of doing** ～する方法 **way to do** ～する方法
- [ ] **weakness** 名①弱さ, もろさ ②欠点, 弱点
- [ ] **web** 名①クモの巣 ②《the W-》ウェブ (=World Wide Web)
- [ ] **weight** 名①重さ, 重力, 体重 ②重荷, 負担 ③重大さ, 勢力 動①重みをつける ②重荷を負わせる
- [ ] **well** 熟as well その上, 同様に **as well as** ～と同様に **do well** うまくいく, 成功する **well -ed**《be -》よく[十分に]～された
- [ ] **well-balanced** 形バランス[釣り合い]のよい, 均衡の取れた
- [ ] **well-being** 名健康で安心なこと, 満足できる生活状態, 幸福
- [ ] **wellness** 名健康であること
- [ ] **what** 熟no matter what たとえ何があろう[起ころう]と **what is possible** 何が[どこまで]できるのか
- [ ] **whatever** 代①《関係代名詞》～するものは何でも ②どんなこと[もの]が～とも 形①どんな～でも ②《否定文・疑問文で》少しの～も, 何らかの

153

□ **WhatsApp** 名 ワッツアップ《メッセージングおよび通話利用サービスの商標》

□ **when to** いつ～すべきか

□ **whenever** 接 ①～するときはいつでも，～するたびに ②いつ～しても

□ **wherever** 接 どこでも，どこへ[で]～するとも 副 いったいどこへ[に・で]

□ **whether** 接 ～かどうか，～かまたは…，～であろうとなかろうと

□ **while** 熟 for a while しばらくの間，少しの間

□ **whoever** 代 ～する人は誰でも，誰が～しようとも

□ **whole** 形 全体の，すべての，完全な，満～，丸～ 名《the－》全体，全部

□ **whom** 代 ①誰を[に] ②《関係代名詞》～するところの人，そしてその人を

□ **whomever** 代 whoeverの目的格

□ **wide** 形 幅の広い，広範囲の，幅が～ある 副 広く，大きく開いて

□ **willing** 形 ①喜んで～する，～しても構わない，いとわない ②自分から進んで行う

□ **wisdom** 名 知恵，賢明（さ）

□ **wise** 形 賢明な，聡明な，博学の

□ **with** 熟 agree with（人）に同意する begin with ～で始まる，～から始める caught up with ～にとらわれる，～のとりこになる do with one's life 人生を費やす filled with《be－》～でいっぱいになる get along with（人）と仲良くする，歩調を合わせる get in touch with ～に触れる，感じる go ahead with〔計画・仕事などを〕進める help ～ with …… …を～の面で手伝う keep up with ～に遅れずについていく，歩調を合わせる play with ～で遊ぶ，～と一緒に遊ぶ stay with ～に耐える［持ちこたえる］ with all ～がありながら，あらゆる～をこめて with ease 容易に，やすやす

すと with joy 喜んで

□ **within** 前 ①～の中[内]に，～の内部で ②～以内で，～を越えないで 副 中[内]へ[に]，内部に 名 内部

□ **wonder** 動 ①不思議に思う，（～に）驚く ②（～かしらと）思う 名 驚き（の念），不思議なもの

□ **work** 熟 at work 働いて，仕事中で work out うまくいく，考え出す，～の結果になる

□ **working** 動 work（働く）の現在分詞 形 働く，作業の，実用的な

□ **world** 熟 all over the world 世界中に in the world 世界で

□ **worried** 動 worry（悩む）の過去，過去分詞 形 心配そうな，不安げな worried about《be－》（～のことで）心配している，～が気になる[かかる]

□ **worry about** ～のことを心配する

□ **worth** 形 （の）価値がある，（～）しがいがある 名 価値，値打ち

□ **worthiness** 名 価値，値打ち，財産

□ **worthy** 形 価値のある，立派な

□ **would like** ～がほしい

□ **would like to** ～したいと思う

□ **Would you like to ～?** ～をしたいですか。

□ **wound** 名 傷 動 ①負傷させる，（感情を）害する ②wind（巻く）の過去，過去分詞

□ **write down** 書き留める

□ **writing** 動 write（書く）の現在分詞 名 ①書くこと，作文，著述 ②筆跡 ③書き物，書かれたもの，文書

□ **wrong** 熟 go wrong 失敗する，道を踏みはずす

Y

□ **year** 熟 for ～ years ～年間，～年

にわたって

□ **yearning** 名憧れ, 切なる思い, 切望

□ **yet** 熟 and yet それなのに, それにもかかわらず

□ **yoga** 名ヨガ

.

English Conversational Ability Test
国際英語会話能力検定

● E-CATとは…
英語が話せるようになるための
テストです。インターネット
ベースで、30分であなたの発
話力をチェックします。

www.ecatexam.com

● iTEP®とは…
世界各国の企業、政府機関、アメリカの大学
300校以上が、英語能力判定テストとして採用。
オンラインによる90分のテストで文法、リー
ディング、リスニング、ライティング、スピー
キングの5技能をスコア化。iTEP®は、留学、就
職、海外赴任などに必要な、世界に通用する英
語力を総合的に評価する画期的なテストです。

www.itepexamjapan.com

ラダーシリーズ

100 Keys for Hope 自分を幸せにする英語100

2022年7月4日　第1刷発行
2024年7月11日　第3刷発行

著　者　ヴィッキー・ベネット

発行者　賀川　洋

発行所　IBCパブリッシング株式会社
　　　　〒162-0804 東京都新宿区中里町29番3号
　　　　菱秀神楽坂ビル
　　　　Tel. 03-3513-4511　Fax. 03-3513-4512
　　　　www.ibcpub.co.jp

印　刷　株式会社シナノパブリッシングプレス
装　丁　伊藤　理恵
イラスト　杉山　薫里

落丁本・乱丁本は、小社宛にお送りください。送料小社負担にてお取り替えいたします。本書の無断複写(コピー)は著作権法上での例外を除き禁じられています。

Printed in Japan
ISBN978-4-7946-0716-4